~

"This story is a prime example of a mother and father going above and beyond to help save their little boy. They will stop at nothing to make sure their child gets the best care and life that he deserves. I am honored to be a part of this amazing boy's journey as one of his healthcare providers."

- KELSEY ORTIZ, REGISTERED NURSE

"LIFE CHANGING. Kristin's story of hope helps you persevere through obstacles you face in life with a positive mental attitude. If you don't believe in miracles, you will when you are done with this book!"

- KRISTY CIKOWSKI, SOCIAL MEDIA SPECIALIST

"There are no words to describe the strength, optimism, and inspiration surrounding Nixon's journey. This little boy has defied all odds and only keeps fighting, while along his way, proving many in the healthcare field wrong. His mother and father are prime examples of pure love, positivity and persistence. I am humbled to be a part of Nixon's healthcare team as his acupuncturist, and blessed to be able to see him on a regular basis. Inspiring is an understatement, as I have seen Nixon and his family go through many ups and downs. However, this beautiful little soul always rises above all expectations. The story of Nixon and his family, as described in this book, is a must read, hopeful, uplifting, and most of all, courageous."

- CHRISTINA GUTHRIE, LICENSED ACUPUNCTURIST AND OWNER OF EASTERN VITALITY ACUPUNCTURE, INC.

~

"This is an inspirational, motivational, and touching story of an average American family. It will change your outlook on life and make you think twice before taking anything for granted. It will remind you to trust your instincts and emphasize to you that anything is possible with hard work, dedication and most importantly, hope. As a mother of three healthy children, I find myself, like most mothers, in denial that anything bad could ever happen to them. This story of Nixon's journey has opened my eyes to reality, and the fact that no one, no matter who you are, is exempt from a devastating event that could turn your life upside down."

- JAMIE COAN, EDUCATOR

"This journey is a moving account of love and strength. This story is courageous and inspiring, as it faces the most heartbreaking challenges that life offers when the Skenderi family learns of their infant son's rare disease. This is a powerful testimony of one couple's love, courage and determination to never give up. I'm honored to have the opportunity to share part of their journey with them and their beautiful son, Nixon, as they fight each day for his survival."

- LINDA PALLER, REGISTERED NURSE

"An awe inspiring, up close and personal story of a young family as they navigate the world with an infant diagnosed with an extremely rare disease. Their courage and never-ending strength has forever changed my definition of hope and what it means to be humble."

- LAURA DURAVA, RETIRED CHIEF OPERATING OFFICER

# holding hope in our hands

A profound, true story to trust your instincts, push for more options, live for a smile and never, ever give up!

KRISTIN SKENDERI

Fig Factor Media LLC

Edited by Cindy Tschosik of SoConnected LLC
Cover Design and Layout by Carrie Keppner
Photography by Josh Dreyfus

Grateful acknowledgment is made to the following for permission to reprint previously published material:

A quote from Jay Neugenboren on page 55.
Reprinted with permission of the author.

Lexi Griffin Behrndt: "An Open Letter to My Son's Medical Team" by Lexi Griffin Behrndt. Reprinted with permission of the author.

Printed and bound in the U.S.A.

ISBN # 978-0-9990012-3-3

In memory of

 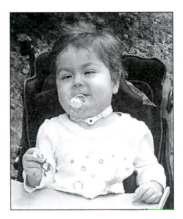

Joseph Edilio DeFacci      Breighlin Olivia Isitt

Photos courtesy of the DeFacci and Isitt families.

# Contents

# Foreword

"A PARENT'S LOVE KNOWS NO BOUNDS," but in my profession, I witness how frequently only parents can truly understand the depth of that commitment.

I have had the privilege of being Nixon Skenderi's Pediatrician for the past two and a half years. His parents are an amazing couple, and I have come to regard them as friends. This book simply and emotionally outlines the struggles and sacrifices that the family endured through Nixon's medical diagnosis, evaluations, testing and treatments. I believe that parents frequently make choices, emotionally, physically, and financially without regard for the long term consequences to themselves. As this book demonstrates, Nixon's parents have literally sacrificed everything, including their home and financial stability. They firmly believe that Nixon is a significant individual and deserves so much more than was ordained for him. They refused to give up even when the odds and the Medical Community seemed against them. Through all the challenges, they maintained a close, loving, and mutually respectful relationship. When they completely disagreed, they never denigrated the other or their view point. This is a lesson for all those who want to maintain a healthy relationship.

Parents love their child unconditionally. They don't see the illness as a disability, but as something to face and conquer as much as possible, even if only through shear will and persistence. They fully believe that their job is to protect their child and "fix" any problems that befall them. In reality, they frequently can't, and I wish they could relieve themselves of the guilt that they caused or could have prevented the issues. When significant issues arise, parents lose their innocence, as well as, their previous joys, hopes, and dreams. They become unwitting "experts" about medicine and medical procedures concerning their loved one.

Successful collaboration is the ultimate goal. The medical professional should accept the family as part of the team, instead of an inconvenience or an obstacle. Even if there is disagreement, be respectful and acknowledge their concerns, opinions, hopes, and dreams. The Skenderis formed alliances with many medical communities and professionals, which optimized Nixon's care and quality of life.

Each person who reads this book will develop their own perspective. The theme is easily recognizable to many who are dealing with a chronic or life altering illness. The story line is impactful, and I hope the reader will come to understand that the situations they face are not their fault. They did not cause it; they did not contribute to it; and they could not have prevented it.

**Frank Roemisch, M.D., F.A.A.P.**
**Pediatrician**

# Preface

I<small>F YOU ARE A PARENT WITH A HEALTHY CHILD</small> and consider yourself to have a "normal" life, please be grateful and do not take that for granted. Hug your kids. Appreciate good health always. A friend's great-grandmother shared with me, "If you have your health, you have everything." It is so very true. I started this journey without knowing anything different. I found myself to be very naïve. I knew there were sick children in this world, but I never knew to this extent. I never knew or acknowledged the astounding number of children that are suffering; nor could I have ever comprehended the level of illness some children endure. I certainly never thought it would or could ever happen to my child. It happened, out of the blue from nowhere, without a warning, without a manual, without anything. From the first second we discovered that our six-month-old baby boy was not healthy, everything changed. Every thought, every day, every evening, every plan, every part of our life changed. Permanently. Our life and our plans for the future were replaced with the new path that was laid ahead for us. My son, my husband and I stepped forward to endure this new life. The three of us together, holding hands, grabbing on for life. Literally. This was our new life absorbed with our worst possible fear, all of our love, and all of our hope.

# Acknowledgements

THANK YOU, OZZIE, for going on this journey with me. Nixon was given to us for a reason, and that is because you and I make an incredible team. We have it harder than most, but somehow we make it all work. The cards were shuffled. In a million years, I would never had thought this would be the life we would be dealt. But I have to say that so far, I think we have played our cards right. I couldn't imagine going through this with anyone else. Look where we started, and look where we are now. We always knew what we wanted to do the minute that we decided to fight this. And that is what we will always continue to do; to never ever give up.

Thank you to my mom and dad who raised me right. The universe knew what it was doing when it put me in your arms. Anytime I have needed you, you have been there in a blink of an eye. You guided me through life and helped me learn to follow my heart. I have strength because of you. You have always believed in me and because of that I feel like I can do anything.

Thank you to my best girlfriends, the extra sisters that I chose for myself; my soul sisters. Good friends are hard to find, but once you find them, you have them for the rest of your life. Not sure what I would do without you. I'm lucky to have you in my life. You helped me remember the important things when I felt I had lost them. My smile, my hope, and my courage.

Thank you to my family and friends for all of your support, love and generosity that you have bountifully shared throughout these challenging years. The power of a support system does wonders, and your support helped Ozzie and me more than you know. The fact that we have had so many people on our side means the world. We will never be able to thank you enough!

Thank you to Nixon's entire medical team: Dr. Maria Escolar, Dr. Mark Vanderlugt, Dr. Frank Roemisch, the NDRD clinic, the BMT staff, the Peds, PICU, and Respiratory teams that we visited at every hospital, all of the fabulous nurses that have taken amazing care of Nixon, his therapists, and to his Journey Care team. I'm thankful that you gave him a chance. You helped save his life and made him as comfortable as possible every day. You believed in us, and you gave us hope. We will never forget you and will be forever grateful.

Thank you to Cindy Tschosik, Carrie Keppner, and Jackie Camacho Ruiz. "The Dream Team." Nixon had a story to tell, and you helped bring it to life. Your talents are incredible, and I'm so happy that my path led me to all of you. You helped make this book what it is.

Last but certainly not least, thank you to Nixon Matthew. You have changed my life. This was all you; I was just your voice through the whole journey. You have done the impossible and have shown so many people that there is nothing in this world that you can't do. Do not ever let anyone tell you differently. You are my heart, you are my soul, and you are the love of my life.

# Introduction

EVERYONE DESERVES A CHANCE. My name is Nixon Matthew Skenderi, and I deserve a chance. That gloomy, rainy day in April of 2014 will be etched in Mommy and Daddy's minds for the rest of their lives. I was a normal six-month-old boy with a full head of dark brown hair and a smile that melted everyone's hearts. I had this little raspy cough that wouldn't go away. Concerned, my parents bundled me up and ventured to the doctor. As my pediatrician performed his usual exam, he noticed that I was not thriving as I should, and I was not meeting the usual growth chart milestones.

He immediately admitted us to the hospital for a barrage of tests that consisted of blood work, ultrasounds of my organs, visual and neurological reaction tests and a bone marrow biopsy. As we were playing with my toys, two doctors entered my hospital room. With one abstract sentence, Mommy and Daddy's world turned upside down. "Your six-month-old son has Gaucher's (gō'SHāz) disease." Mayo-Clinic defines it as "the result of a buildup of certain fatty substances in certain organs, particularly the spleen and liver. This causes these organs to become much larger than normal and can affect their function." The doctors explained it to Mommy, Daddy and me,

"This is a genetic, fast progressing lysosomal storage disease, which lacks an enzyme in the body that causes children to become disabled and not live past the age of three. It is extremely rare. It is fatal and has no cure." No cure. No cure. No cure.

In three confusing sentences, we fell swirling into a black hole. In translation, Gaucher's disease, enlarges many of my organs, affects my breathing, restricts my swallowing and limits my neurological development.

They say bad news happens in threes, and our small family has had our fair share. It started before I was born and before they were even married. In 2007, daddy was attacked while walking home from a night out in Chicago. He was hit over the head with a construction hammer and almost lost his life. He survived and lived to be the strong, loving, amazing daddy I know him to be today. In 2011, mommy turned her head the wrong way and tore her carotid artery. It caused her to have a mini stroke. The doctors said she should have been in a vegetative state, but she's not. She is as energetic, brave and inspiring as any mommy I know. They were both given miraculous second chances. Then I was born, and it is the most joyous time in their lives. And now, this happens to me.

I may never be able to say "Mommy" or "Daddy." I may never crawl or walk, go to school, have my first kiss, graduate, get married, nor see the world. It's not fair. It's not fair that I may not get a chance to live all of our dreams. Does good news happen in threes, too? Why is this happening? Why us? The truth is, why not us?

My mom and dad have taken this by storm, of course. They love me! They have spoken to almost every expert and doctor in the U.S. who knows of Gaucher's disease. Each conversation ends with the doctor or expert saying, "there is no real hope."

Doctors have been working on a treatment to help other babies like me, but any hope of a cure is still years away. Unfortunately, it doesn't look like they will have a breakthrough in the next few months.

In an effort to slow the process down, we quickly started the most aggressive treatment available. It is only meant to help me feel comfortable. My treatment will become an all-day enzyme replacement therapy, which will be administered through an IV every two weeks. Physical therapy will help strengthen me, so I can hold my head up and roll over.

Regardless of the outcome, I don't want mommy and daddy to be sad. I have this life with them, and they are the best mommy and daddy I could ever ask for. They show me and teach me as much of the world as they possibly can. I get to smile and laugh. I get to do things that, unfortunately, some other children don't. I was given the chance to meet my family. Mommy and Daddy are going to make the best of this horrible situation. They are going to give me all the love that I can get. And they will truly enjoy the best of me.

April, 2014

WE DID THIS. Ozzie and I did this to our son. Not intentionally, of course, but it was the irritatingly wrong way that our genes mixed. Now, Nix doesn't have a chance.

We have been at a local hospital in the suburbs of Chicago since last Thursday, six days ago. For what seems like eternity, our time has been spent completing extensive testing and many meetings with both doctors and specialists. The MRI of his brain was normal. Yes! The biopsy of his bone marrow, showed abnormal cells. No! This test determined that Nixon is diagnosed with Gaucher's (gō'SHāz) Disease. For the 30 years that my husband and I have been on this earth, we have never heard of it. This disease is inherited and is completely genetic. Certain genes, when combined, create a deficiency in the glucocerebrosidase enzyme that your body needs to survive. THERE IS NO CURE. THERE IS NO CURE. THERE IS NO CURE.

How can that be? It is 2014 in the United States of America! How do we process that? What does that mean? Do we have to live with those words? Is that really what is going to happen? A million questions swirled through our minds. This can't be possible.

As any parent, we jumped to our most "reliable" source, the internet. We needed to find out as much about this disease as we could. We learned that there are three types of this disease. If anyone must live with this, Type 1 offers the best outcome of a full life. Type 2 is the worst, and Type 3 is a slower progressing version of Type 2.

In Types 2 and 3, Gaucher's Disease symptoms generally appear in infancy or early childhood. Well, we can roll the dice on this one, but let's face the fact that Nixon is six-months-old. This can manifest itself with abnormally slow eye movements, unsteadiness in balance, swallowing problems, seizures, and other symptoms. Neurological involvement ranges from minimal to severe. Are you kidding me? He is our first child. What are the odds that this could happen? One in a million. Seriously, one in a million. At this point, we don't know Nix's Type. Next up: DNA tests to determine the type. The results will be back in about a week. A week? Really? All this information is mind-boggling. A few days ago, we had a healthy son. A lingering cough, a doctor's visit and an admission to the hospital changed everything. Within 24-hours and six days later, we are in the throws of the worst possible fear that any parent can imagine. No child should have to experience the possibility of death and no parent should have to watch their child die. My heart hurts.

Regardless of the type, Gaucher patients can receive enzyme replacement infusions every other week for the rest of their lives to keep comfortable. Okay, well there is a small temporary solution. Not a cure, but it's something. The caveat is that the replacement enzyme has difficulty getting to the brain in Types 2 and 3. It needs to reach the brain to help the rest of the body function properly. It said difficulty, but it didn't say it was impossible. A sliver of hope.

This morning, we met with our team of doctors and specialists. Due to Nixon exhibiting the symptoms early, in infancy, he could have Type 2. If this is the case, he needs enzyme replacements every other week. "He will start to lose function of his brain. He could have a short life of two to three years."

Most parents would be sobbing hysterically after hearing this. I, on the other hand was stoic. I don't know if it was because I was in denial, if I just didn't believe it, or if it was just because a small part of me just had a feeling that regardless of what the doctors were telling me, I knew it wasn't going to be the end for him. I was ready to fight. I was ready to research my ass off and do whatever it would take to make my precious baby okay.

Determined to learn more and find answers, my fingers marched back to the all-knowing internet. I had read about the disease as a whole, but I needed to read more about just Type 2.

*According to Healthtap.com, "Type 2 Gaucher's disease has the earliest onset, within the first 3 to 6 months of life, and it is fatal; causing death before 2 years of age. Due to the shortened lifespan, babies with Type 2 will not survive long enough to develop some symptoms experienced by individuals with Type 1 and Type 3."*[1]

Am I really reading this? They will prepare us for the worst, but we must still hope for the best. This could still be Type 1, which means a full life with enzyme replacements every other week. Or maybe, Type 3, which would give time for someone to find a cure. Tonight, they will release us from the hospital and we are going home to get a change of scenery. This is too much to digest.

Tomorrow is Nixon's six-month birthday. By this time, most parents are watching their children army crawl around their house and hearing the babbles of "mama and dada." We, on the other hand, are planning how to spend the rest of Nixon's possibly very short life. I need a distraction. Hello social media, my good friend. Hold on. Maybe not a good idea, as I read and scroll through to see other parents bragging about their children's milestones. Rightfully so, because I probably would do the same thing. A few friends of mine had children around the same time that we did. I love their kids so much. As happy as I am that their kids are starting these milestones, it breaks my heart. I don't know if my son will ever get to experience any of them. It makes me jealous; it makes me sad; and I wish I didn't feel this way. Ozzie and I are trying to stay as strong as possible for him, but that's not saying much. I feel like I'm living in a nightmare, and I can't wake up. This is, by far, the hardest thing that we have ever had to deal with and something that no one should deal with. But we are fighters, and regardless of the outcome, we will continue to fight through this and give Nixon the best possible life that we can.

> *"We all want to grow up in this amazing life that we were given the chance to live. I'm not going to rely on the medicine because that isn't where breakthroughs come from. They come from the people who never give up. And I'm going to find the breakthrough that Nixon needs."*
> – KRISTIN SKENDERI

The internet was our best friend for the next days to come. Every day we type "cure for Gaucher's Disease." It has become our daily ritual to read any and every article with a mention of this disease. We want to find and work with the experts, the doctors that spend their life studying this disease. There are not many, maybe a dozen. Gaucher's is rare. As Nixon's parents, no matter what anyone tells us, we are not giving up on him. Ah! Success. "Hello, Doctor... I see. Thank you for the referral."

Each time we talk to one, we receive another name to call. We don't stop. Each one will be contacted, either by phone or email. The doctor in Israel has to be our lucky contact. He's a scientist who has been working on a cure. "If this cure were to work, it is still years in the making. I'm sorry."

Why are each of these doctors telling us the same story? "We are sorry you are going through this. We know the rough road that you have ahead. Enjoy him. You are a young family, you can have more." Each time, we feel disgusted with those words. It is devastating that the people who devote their lives to studying this disease can't help us. I know they are the experts, but there has to be something that someone can do. Do not tell us that "There is no hope." In this day and age there has to be. There has to be hope.

A glimmer. The doctors at the hospital referred us to a clinic in Cincinnati that specializes in and treats children daily who have this. They help those mostly with Type 3, but have seen some with Type 2. The very next call, and we have an appointment for an evaluation and more information. Time to pack. Ohio, here we come!

Four hours and thirty minutes is the longest trip Nixon has traveled since he was born. We will have hours to reflect on all the devastating news we just received. Through our research, I stumbled upon the Gaucher's Foundation.[2] This should be a wonderful resource. Hopefully, we meet others who are dealing with Gaucher's, just like us.

With hope in our hearts and in my hand as I dial, a gentleman who is one of the main contacts of the foundation answers the phone with a calm and kind voice. He obviously has had this conversation before today. Through his tone and words, I can also hear the uncertainty of our future. Trying not to tremble and cry, I ask, "We are headed to Cincinnati. Do you have any advice to ease our minds?" Him and his wife had a son who passed from this disease a long time ago. They tried a transplant, but he did not survive. Once again, more unanswered questions, rather than hope. The cure is years from now, and while support groups sound nice, we are looking for a way to fix our child. We do not want to join a group of people to help us grieve. However, he did refer a family who lives close to us who went through this with their son. I am looking forward to contacting them once we get home.

While in Ohio, Nixon will be evaluated by four doctors that specialize in this disease. The questions seem endless. How many more times will we need to talk about how and when he started losing his abilities? He is only six-months-old, and there was not much. We once again shared that the only signs were his eyes started crossing, low muscle tone, and he lost the ability to hold himself up in a seal position while being on his tummy. Aside from that, he was doing everything that a normal baby would do. He smiles, laughs, tries to roll over, grabs for his toys, holds his bottle and kicks his legs. In my opinion, he's damn perfect.

"This is a fast progressing disease. Kids around his age lose their ability to swallow and need a tracheal tube for breathing and a G-tube for eating." Is that good news? Is there hope there? Each day, Nixon still remarkably drinks thirty ounces of formula from a bottle. Maybe it's not as bad as it seems since he is doing so well, compared to others. The biopsy results come back, and the doctor confirms the Gaucher's cells are present. Since the cells and indicators are present at his sweet, young age of six months, it is more than likely to be Type 2, rather than 3. The labs will prove their conclusion later this afternoon. Although the odds are stacked against us, and the facts point to Type 2, until I know otherwise, I will still hope for Type 1 or 3. People can live with Type 1 and 3. Why would we be given this beautiful baby just to have him taken away from us?

The rest of the afternoon flies by as we talk to the doctors about Nixon's quality of life over the coming months and hopefully, years. We are talking about the quality of life of a six-month-old. What? Isn't that the conversation you have about your grandparents, parents or even when considering leaving a stressful job? This isn't the way it is supposed to be. When Nixon was born, we had so many hopes and dreams for him. We are only six months into his life. This isn't right. I want to vomit.

The compassionate doctors cautiously step us through the facts. To help his body and central nervous system function, his brain needs the enzyme he lacks. Without it, everything will slowly start to shut down. However, each child is unique and exhibits differently, so we don't know what to expect. The good news is that enzyme replacement therapy (ERT) will help slow the process down as it gives the body the lacking enzyme. This will help all organs from the neck down function the way they should. The problem is, the enzyme cannot get past the blood brain barrier, and therefore it will still cause the brain to eventually shut everything down. The doctor in Israel is trying to find some way to get the enzyme to the brain. Someone other than the one man in Israel must be working on this, right? But if they were, this team of doctors would know about it. We have read about bone marrow transplants, but they have never been proven to work. The doctors advise us there is a 95% chance of not surviving. Transplants are very hard on the body. Since this disease affects the organs it's not a very good idea. Our only option is to make his short life as painless and comfortable as possible. They load us down with many brochures about a drug company that can help. They provide a drug that is used for the enzyme replacement therapy, and it will become a huge part of our daily life. They gave us the name of a pharmaceutical liaison. We don't know it yet, but she becomes our new best friend in this fight for life. I still can't help feeling hopeless.

In a little waiting room, it is dark, suppressing and small. Ozzie, two nurse practitioners and I are discussing the protocol. Knock. Time stopped, and my heart lurched forward and then halted. Whatever words this doctor speaks will change our lives forever.

Holding Nixon's file in his hand, the doctor cautiously walks in the room with his head down. One quick, inquisitive glance at his face, and I knew. He starts. He hesitates. No, please. Don't hesitate. Every emotion I have left is now numb, and my heart breaks into a million pieces. With his southern accent, he softly speaks very slowly in terms that we understand because he knows he is sharing extremely heavy news.

"Nixon has either a slow progressing form of Type 2 or a more aggressive version of Type 3. Either way, it is the neuronopathic version, and the enzyme is not getting to his brain." There isn't a chance that Nixon will live a long happy life and all of our worst nightmares are coming true. No hope.

On their hands, the doctors counted how many known children were being treated for this version. My body freezes. Nothing they say now matters because our entire life is now upside down. Emotions swirl violently through our minds, words, and movements. We don't understand why this is happening. "If there was a cure, we would know about it. Stop trying to do research. Focus on Nixon."

The halls are endless and our legs are heavy as we maneuver through the clinic to our car. We find ourselves at a park close to our hotel. Holding Nixon's hand, we journey through the park. Nix and I climb the steps to the slide, I snuggle him into my chest and hold him securely. If a mother's hold could save a child, he would be saved by that one trip down the slide. My tears fall before we land on the mulch pit and a huge smile takes over Nixon's face. His infectious smile lights up the world, and grabs my entire heart every time I see it. His love radiates from it, and no matter the circumstance, it makes my soul feel alive again. I cradle his little body in the swing and push as that smile remains. He is as carefree as can be and has no idea what is going on. I want to keep it that way. Everything inside of me needs out. Ozzie's mind was not there either. Tears were streaming down his face, and he was holding onto Nixon as he went down the slide with him. He could think of nothing else but the devastating news we just heard. He felt absolutely helpless. We just need to at least try to digest everything before we leave for home.

Home. How do we cherish these moments? How many do we have left? What moments do we create? Where is the book on "Moments to Live When There is No Hope?"

I replay our actions up to that point. We have contacted everyone that we felt we could contact regarding this disease. We said we wouldn't give up. Easier to say than do when you have no idea of the next step. We don't know where else to turn. I really can't wrap my head around any of this. My child did nothing to himself to deserve this. He just happened to end up with this illness out of pure dumb luck.

As Ozzie and Nixon sleep, seemingly peaceful and comfortable, I open my email. The first one up is an email from my boss's daughter.

*Kristin, Ozzie and Nixon,*
*There are not many words that I can say. I hope you know that I love you all. Nixon has something special. His life will be filled with nothing but LOVE. His whole life will be love and good people around him. His innocence and smile are Eternal. I can't tell you that this will make sense someday. SCREW THAT. This is unfair and the biggest load of bullshit. However, as a family, you get the chance to ignore the real bullshit and take this time to love each other and relish in it. I guess in all of the dark, I hope your time together will be the light.*

I read it again. And again. And again.

On the drive home, I remember there is one person we have left to contact. She is a leading geneticist at a medical research center. As we talked for an hour, it sounded like much of the same. In one ear, out the other. Except for one thing, one harsh thing that was said and unfortunately has stuck with us since. "You are a young family. You can have more kids." I disconnect the phone. Stunned. I look to Ozzie. Ozzie looks at me. Pained. Hurting. Shocked. Stunned. Then we both take one look at Nixon and cry for the rest of the ride home. We knew at that point, there was no hope.

We need to do everything we possibly can to slow this process down and enjoy him as best as we can. I call the team of doctors at a hospital in downtown Chicago to start the process for enzyme replacement therapy and insurance approval for the oral medication usually prescribed to Type 1 patients. They are willing to try it with Nixon. As we hope and pray every day for a miracle, we want Nixon to see and do everything and anything we can possibly offer him in this world. A miracle is the only thing that will save him at this point. What should we do first? The cure for any sadness and the place where dreams come true... Disneyland! Watch out, Mickey, we are coming next month! Nixon can't wait to meet you!

Back in Chicago, we try our best to get back into our normal routine. While Ozzie is at work, he receives a call from the liaison for the new enzyme replacement drug company. The phone call that we have been expecting. As he speaks with her, he realizes she is one of the friendliest and most helpful people that Ozzie has ever encountered. Relief settles in as she claims she is going to help our family with so much. She explains the benefits she can offer our family while Nixon would receive their drug. In addition, all kinds of support and even a $10,000 cash stipend to help with travel expenses. They are going to provide medical equipment as needed along with an entire laundry list of all good things. It seems strange, but we figure this is our new reality.

Soon after the call, we head down to the hospital in Chicago to begin the ERT. It was about an hour drive on a beautiful spring day. The sun really makes a difference. On a nerve-wracking day of not really knowing what to expect, the sunshine gives me a sense of calmness. Like chemotherapy, the enzyme is administered through an IV, while sitting in a chair for a few hours. It takes four hours to complete the treatment, and a few hours to monitor him. This will continue every two weeks, but the more ERT treatments Nixon receives, the time will shorten to hopefully one to two hours. At some point, a nurse will come to the house to give him his treatments. Eventually, they will give him a port, so he won't get poked so many times with a needle. I remember how hard it was watching him receive his immunizations. I always cringe when the nurse inserts the needle. At this point, it is commonplace for Ozzie and me to see Nixon getting poked with needles. It's starting to not even phase him. The worst part is when they tie that rubber band around him to stop the blood flow.

With medical treatments, come medical bills. We are still battling with insurance, but we hope he will start his oral medication soon. The ERT costs around $200,000 per year. We received approval to start six continuous treatments.

It seems that hospitals, doctor's visits, exams, needles, tests and therapy will be our new norm. While all of my friends will be having play dates with their kids, we will be spending hours at hospitals. I feel so alone because there isn't anyone in my circle of family or friends that can even relate to this situation.

Then, while I'm sadly reflecting on what I am missing, I recall the family that lives close to us. Their son, also, had Gaucher's. I call Bobbie, the mom, and she agreed to talk with us and meet Nixon. As the day arrives for her visit, I feel so anxious because

I have no idea what she will say. I also feel a sense of relief because she has been through this and can help us get a sense of what is to come. She came to our door. The first thing she wanted to do was hold Nixon. As she holds him, I can tell that this experience is triggering a lot of memories for her.

Her son, Joey, was diagnosed just after his first birthday. Unfortunately, he passed away in the 90's from this horrible disease. She shared how he was affected from when he was diagnosed until he passed. As I listen to her share her story, I am overwhelmed by her strength. He was just a little over 3 years old. She said that Nix and Joey shared similar symptoms at six-months-old, but again every person and diagnosis is different. Nixon's experience will not exactly be the same as Joey's.

When she finishes, she tells me she has never met with any other family or discussed in detail what happened with Joey. In our time together, she relived almost every detail she experienced with him up until the day he passed. I know this conversation was extremely hard for her, and she shared it with so much grace. I am grateful to know Joey's story. Bobbie now has a seventeen-year-old son who is a carrier, and fortunately, he does not have the disease.

Her visit helps us realize that we are not alone on this journey. She generously offered to lend an extra set of ears since she knows what the doctors are talking about. Over the past 10 years, she reiterates that the experts have made significant progress. Unfortunately for Nix, it doesn't look like they will have a breakthrough in the next few months. Bobbie is the sweetest, most sincere woman I have ever met. It means the world to us that she carved out time in her day to help us prepare for what could come and then also extended herself to help through the coming days, months and years. There is something very special about her. My internal instinct says she will be in our life for a long time.

We start getting back into a normal routine by the middle of May. Although, nothing is normal about our lives. Each day, we feel like we are absolutely failing. The only thing that we know we can do to help Nixon is to give him his ERT treatments. At this point, he has only received two. As much as Ozzie and I want to spend every minute we have with Nixon, we, unfortunately, have to work. We need the insurance and our paychecks. Even though our bodies are sitting at a desk, every second of every day, our minds and hearts are just on Nixon. As I stare at the computer screen, tears roll down my cheeks because I start thinking about taking Nixon to Disneyland.

A few months before conceiving Nix, I had a miscarriage. I couldn't help but wonder why? Why would I lose a baby, then be given this baby just to have him struggle through a short life and be taken away from us? I can't wrap my head around it because it doesn't make any sense. I'm a person who always needs to know the why and how. With this, I don't know if I ever will know those answers. I know it's crazy. After reading every statistic and speaking with every doctor, I know that there is no cure, but I have this feeling that just won't go away. I know that every doctor has told us that nothing can be done. They are the doctors, and I'm just a mom with a 9-5 job. How do I ignore this strong pull in my gut telling me that this just can't be it for him?

The more I think about everything that has happened in the past month, the more pissed off I get. I constantly get this fire inside of me. It's something that keeps insisting that I need to do something other than sit around and watch my precious little man die. I know the odds are stacked against us, but screw the odds. Odds mean crap. We have a choice. We can run away and hide from this, or we can face it. We need to face it, and we need to fight it. I'm not going to give up on this until I find the answers that we need.

Feeling a renewed energy and empowered from that mother's

instinct each of us moms have, I dash off to my most trusted source, the internet. From all of my article readings, I learn that Gaucher's disease is more prominent in people who are Jewish and Eastern European. I type "Cure for Gaucher's Disease Europe." Even though we talked to everyone we could find in the United States, there had to be other people who knew of this disease elsewhere. I read through article after article. Then, my entire body froze and my heart almost stopped. I copied and pasted a link in an email to Ozzie and wrote "Oz, I think these people might be able to help us." Hope is alive. Again.

[1] HealthTap.com. Top 10 Doctor Insights on: Gaucher Disease Early Onset. https://www.healthtap.com/topics/gaucher-disease-early-onset

[2] GaucherDisease.org. *National Gaucher Foundation.* http://www.gaucherdisease.org/

~

"He who has health, has hope; and
he who has hope, has everything."

– Thomas Carlyle

# Two

May, 2014

FEELING AMBITIOUS, Ozzie and I both arrive home from work today and want to discuss our approach from our findings in Europe. I found two professors at a university in the United Kingdom. These two gentlemen developed the oral medication that Nixon needs, and we have been trying to get for him. We don't know how much help they will offer. However, they know Gaucher's, and they are trying to do something about it.

We decide Ozzie will send an email to share our story and tell them about Nixon's diagnosis. We hope through the email, they feel us beg them from the bottom of our hearts for any type of help they can give us. We will even fly to the UK to meet them, if necessary. Waiting for a reply from an email is nerve-wracking, especially when it can possibly hold your child's future in its hands. We won't have to wait long though, as the time difference is in our favor.

To our surprise their response arrives quickly. They sympathize with our distress on receiving Nixon's diagnosis. As they explain that they can't do much themselves, they already forwarded

Ozzie's email to a professor of medicine at a university in England who works with patients who have Gaucher's disease.

Great, now we have to be agonizingly patient for another person to respond via email. Luckily, when we wake up, that email is in Ozzie's inbox!

This doctor shares that in his life, he has seen approximately 160 patients with Gaucher's Disease. Out of that 160, about fifteen children were diagnosed with the condition. He has worked with less than six who have Nixon's type. Bless his heart, his intellect, experience and expertise. He goes on and on about medical information that zooms way over my head. But then he mentions an outside chance that we could explore a stem cell transplant. Wait. What? I stop. I read excitedly again. Hope. It will largely be an experimental procedure in Gaucher's Disease, as they don't know one child with the disease who has survived a transplant. However, if Nixon was severely affected already, it would not be ethical because of the dangers surrounding a transplant for a young and very sick baby. Bingo!!! Nixon has not been severely affected nor is he a very sick baby… yet. Oz replied to his email stating the symptoms that Nixon has, what he has lost and what he is still doing. The doctor replied saying that there is hope. He shared the names of five doctors that could possibly help us. That's what I like to hear… hope. Of these five doctors, only one was in the United States. Pennsylvania. Immediately, Ozzie picks up the phone to contact her.

As we get acquainted over email with Dr. Escolar from Pennsylvania, we learn that she is the director of a program for the study of neurodevelopment in rare disorders. Ozzie explains how we received her information from the professor in the UK and that he recommended us to reach out to her for advice. Once again, he shares all of Nixon's details and how we are very open to any experimental agents, including a stem cell transplant. It is definitely something we want to explore so we can treat this disease as aggressively as possible. And again, we have to wait for an emailed reply. Waiting is the worst part. I definitely prefer knowing because then you can plan. I'm a planner. Then my mind started racing, and my heart started beating so fast. A transplant is a lot to think about. Everyone we have spoken with and every article we have read about it says it's very risky. There isn't any proof that any child with this disease has survived. But I needed to hear what she had to say. Just from the title of her occupation I knew that she could maybe help us.

It is a warm sunny Sunday in May. Nixon and I are snuggled on the couch, and I'm reading books to him. Ozzie is at the White Sox game with his brother. My phone buzzes. I read the text, "We are going to the East Coast!" Oh My God! She responded, and it has to be good news. I can't wait until he comes home with all of the details.

Really? I have to wait? This is something for which my husband is notorious. He sends me very vague text messages that leave me on the edge of my seat. I hate that men are not detail-oriented.

The second he walks in the door, four hours later, I grab his phone to read the email. She suggests we come there for a consultation. When we are there, they will evaluate Nixon's condition in more detail to see if he would benefit from an umbilical cord stem cell transplant. She explains that it is very rare that babies are diagnosed soon enough, but she mentions that it looks like Nixon may still be on time. She stressed how important the timing is and asked how soon we could be there. The first flight available is Tuesday. We are going to Pennsylvania to see if our son has a chance! For the first time in over a month, my emotions turn from heartbroken, terrified, and numb to some actual excitement. Tuesday won't come soon enough.

The flight to Pennsylvania is literally only a little over an hour; a perfect flight for an anxious couple with a six-month-old baby.

On the flight, Ozzie shares with me some concerns about his new liaison friend from the pharmaceutical company. He can't help but wonder why a company is so helpful and so willing to dish out all this money to keep our son on a drug that isn't even going to cure his disease. Something about that phone call is really eating at him. Being the pessimistic person that he is, he is starting to feel used and betrayed. "Why did we have to go through so many obstacles to realize that we only have to go to Pennsylvania?" It is ridiculous that a simple email from someone thousands of miles away, in England, was the catalyst to get us here now.

Anyone who has been to Chicago knows that the weather is completely unpredictable. Our plane pulled into Pittsburgh International Airport on Wednesday. Yes, I said Wednesday because our Tuesday flight was cancelled due to thunderstorms all day long. Luckily, the compassionate and dedicated doctors who wanted to meet and examine Nixon were able to push back his appointments until we arrived.

Landed. Now, off to the hotel to drop off luggage and right to the hospital. Wow. What a site. From the street view, the hospital is huge and majestic as it rests on a hill showcasing its colorful bricks of purple, orange and blue. It could be its own city. It brings me a bit of joy knowing that we are going to such a beautiful place that does such amazing work – helping save children's lives.

As we walk through the front doors, I can't even define how my nerves are firing off everywhere. With eyes wide open, I am surrounded by children, parents, doctors, nurses and volunteers. As they walk by me, I am overwhelmed because despite what these experts tell us about Nixon, I know I will be seeing a lot of hospital lobbies in our near future.

As we approach the check-in counter, we receive our badges

and name tags. I like this – a secure hospital. With name badges affixed, we solemnly walk to the room to meet the doctor and her team. Immediately, they take Nixon's vitals and get started with the exam. This is it. The beginning of what could possibly change Nixon's life forever. Vitals and exams are nothing to this kid now. He just smiles and waves his toys. He loves seeing new people so it gives me comfort knowing this is somewhat exciting for him. If he only knew...

We muddle through the next three days as if in a vacuum. All the activity humming around us is obvious, but I feel like I'm living outside my body. They evaluate Nixon to see if his body is healthy enough for the transplant. Right after vitals, he has an Auditory Brainstem Response Evaluation. This gives information about the inner ear and brain pathways for hearing. Tomorrow, the Nerve Conduction Velocity test will identify how fast electrical signals move through a nerve. On the third day of our visit, Friday, he will have a Visual Evoked Potential. Nixon will sit in front of a screen that displays an alternating checkerboard pattern to measure the activity in certain areas of the brain. For now, the final test, will be a brain MRI/Spinal Tap, while under general anesthesia. I hate having to put him through all of that testing, especially anesthesia. In 33 years, I have never been under anesthesia, and Nixon who isn't even one yet will have to experience it. After the three days, the results of the tests come in. They show that Nixon did great, understandably fussy at times, but overall, he did what they needed.

Finally, it's late afternoon on Friday, Ozzie's birthday, and we get to meet with the head doctor on the team. She is the one person in this world that can possibly give us the hope that we need. As we sit in the waiting room, anxious doesn't even begin to describe our mental, physical and emotional state. I'm completely terrified. Our email pal, the nurse practitioner, walks in with paperwork and checks all of Nixon's vitals again. She escorts us into a small room with a mat, double sided mirrors and different therapy toys. We sit down and wait. Thirty minutes passes and in walks Dr. Escolar who will make the decision on Nixon's possible transplant. She is a tall, beautiful, confident, intellectual, Colombian woman with long dark hair.

"Thank you for giving us the chance to see you. We are more grateful than you know." She remarks that Nixon is an absolute doll. She patiently, intently and carefully observes Nixon's responses to the work the different therapists perform on his gross and fine motor skills. Her analysis will determine the skill level he has reached versus his current age. Luckily, at almost seven-months-old, his fine motor skills are not that far behind. However, Nixon's gross motor skills adjusted his age to a three-month level.

Nixon has always marched to the beat of his own drum, so getting him to do what they wanted was a bit of a struggle. However, they were able to gather enough of an assessment for the evaluation. Afterwards, Dr. Escolar sits down with us and explains that during her career, she has evaluated a few children with Gaucher's Disease. Unfortunately, she had to turn them down for the transplant because she did not believe it would help them. She continued to say out of anyone, Nixon is healthy enough and is a viable candidate to go through an umbilical cord stem cell transplant. She believes it will work in his favor.

At this moment, my heart that had been broken into a million pieces more than once, just starts to piece itself back together again. With the rarity and fatality of this disease, she is hand picking my child to go through a procedure that could save him. At this hospital, they have never transplanted a child with Gaucher's disease. Nixon will be the first. As she teaches us about the process, she explains that there is a possibility that any abilities he lost or any ability he happens to lose during the process will not come back. For example, if he loses his ability to grab things, he may not gain that back.

After she kindly and thoroughly explains Nixon's chances, she leaves the room. A few minutes later, she returns with the transplant doctor, Dr. Mark, who explains to us what the transplant he will entail. Ironically, he looks like he is my age. He is tall and thin, and he reminds me of some of my friends back home. As I intently watch and listen to both of them, I can't help but think how is this man, who is my age, going to possibly save Nixon's life?

At this point, these two people were our only hope, so I must at least listen. His voice was soft and patient as he explained the entire process from beginning to end. It is extremely hard on the body. If we choose this route, they want us to be prepared for what is to come. Until then, we had been told by numerous doctors that if Nixon would have a transplant, he would have a 95% chance of not making it. From their vantage point, they explained that those doctors had it backwards. If we do nothing, he will have a 0% chance of life. If we do the ERT treatment, he would have a small chance at a short life. If we do a transplant he would have a 95% chance at life and possibly, a full one.

Transplants are still risky because many things can go wrong like graft versus host disease, which is when the body starts to reject the new cells that he is given. But I can't think of the worst. This could be Nixon's chance, his only chance. I know there are risks, but this may be a risk that we will have to take. I looked at Dr. Mark with tears in my eyes, my voice quivers as I say, "You do realize, that if this does work," and then I can't say another word. He continues my sentence, "we could save his life." And the tears flowed down my face. That was the first time I had heard a doctor say that they could save his life, and that is when I knew. But he said that if it were to work, we didn't have time. The process needed to start as soon as possible. If we do this, we need to be back in two weeks. The entire transplant process can take between five and eight months. There are some feelings that refuse to go away, like a little distraction that rings in your ear. You can try, but you can't ignore your instincts. Well, my instinct was screaming "Pennsylvania."

On the way to the hotel, Ozzie and I barely say a word to each other. I want to know what he is thinking, and I know he wants to know what I am thinking. I had so much going through my head at that moment that it even hurt to think. We decide to try to eat at the hotel restaurant. Finally, at dinner, Ozzie breaks the silence by saying, "I think it's a no brainer." I can't agree with him more. It's exactly like the doctors put it; if we are to do this then he has a chance. In the beginning, we said that, we would not give up on him. If we did not try this, then we couldn't live with ourselves knowing, "what if?" We had to do it. We were going to do it. Holy cow, we were going to move to Pennsylvania to give our son a chance at this life!

We walk into the lobby to use the computer. The few people who know where we are want an update. Ozzie looks and me, and says "Do you really want to do this?" I reply, "One thousand percent." We sit down together and write a mass email to all our close family and friends. Since it is Ozzie's birthday, I let him write it.

*First of all, from the bottom of our hearts, we cannot think of the correct words to thank all of you enough for the amount of support and generosity we have received from all of you. Many of you might not even know where we are, and we had to do that for a reason; but now we wanted to give everyone an update.*

*Sometimes, a parent's drive and survival instinct kicks in and overrides what 99.9% of what doctors may say. Kristin and I have worked daily, hours on end, searching for a miracle for Nixon. And believe it or not, on my birthday today (May 29th), we have found that .1% of a doctor that thinks like us. Any birthday wish I could ever imagine was granted today.*

*We have been in Pennsylvania, working with some of the most brilliant doctors I have ever spoken with in my life. They have agreed that Nixon would be a good candidate for an umbilical cord stem cell transplant. As most of you know, we have spoken to many medical professionals around the world regarding this horrible disease, and we have fought our way to where we are now, creating our own luck for Nixon.*

*On Saturday, Kristin, Nixon and I will be home where we will rest for about two to three weeks before returning to Pennsylvania to begin our next journey. Our lives will be on hold for the next five to eight months as we win back Nixon's life. The East Coast will be our new home for rest of the year.*

*As a thank you to everyone who has been supporting us and anyone who wants a detailed description of how and why we made this decision, we ask that you join us to see Nixon for a "see you soon and good luck" party this Sunday at Kristin's parents' house at 12:00pm.*

*We love you all, and thank you for everything!*

*Ozzie, Kristin and Nixon*

~

"The most difficult thing is the decision to act, the rest is merely tenacity. The fears are paper tigers. You can do anything you decide to do. You can act to change and control your life; and the procedure, the process is its own reward."

– Amelia Earhart

# Three

Saturday, May 31, 2014

WE ARE BACK HOME in Chicago with a plan of action. Tomorrow, we meet with all of our family and friends at my parent's house. We know it will be good for us, and it is exactly what we need. We need to be around the people who love us because it's going to be the toughest fight of our lives. We won't be able to do it alone.

That day, 50 of our family and friends came to support us. Our favorite Italian restaurant, down the street, delivered sandwiches and pizzas. We were surprised and grateful for the generosity extended by our guests. We received gifts, gift cards, and gas cards. Nixon is so loved, and in the grand scheme of things, that is what is most important. I actually took a minute to just stop and look around to relish the moment of all the people who supported us. It means the world. Ozzie and I presented our speech to explain, in detail, everything that we had been through and how we came to make our decision. Everyone in attendance unanimously agreed that we needed to move to Pennsylvania. I finally felt like we were moving in the right direction.

For over 10 years, Ozzie and I have had our jobs. My employer was extremely supportive. Even though I had to resign, they said that when it was all done, they would be happy to have me return, whenever I was ready. It gave me goosebumps. Ozzie's work also was extremely supportive and allowed him to take a leave of absence, so we could keep our insurance. This was very important, and we felt very lucky.

Insurance… shoot. We need to call them now to confirm coverage. We live in Illinois. He is having this procedure done in Pennsylvania. This was next on our next plan of action.

Since we only have 2 weeks to be sure everything is covered by insurance, Ozzie diligently starts calling to ensure Nixon's transplant is covered. Dr. Mark and Dr. Escolar wrote very convincing letters to our insurance company to help them approve the process.

It didn't take long because the next day the email arrives with a denial letter from the insurance company that is also signed by our pediatrician. The letter explains that even though a stem cell transplant is a possible treatment option, it is an experimental therapy for Gaucher's Disease. It is not a covered expense in Nixon's insurance plan. Appalled, I start firing off questions. How is anything ever approved then? There has to be a first time for everything, right? We don't have time to appeal the decision, and we don't know what else to do, so we call the doctors in Pennsylvania to inquire about the price of a transplant. With everything said and done, it's around two million dollars. Yeah… we don't have that. A few zeroes too many. Our family and friends start a fundraiser for us. Shocked by this generous offer, Ozzie and I can't seem to know how to react. We have never accepted money because we always have been hard workers and do everything ourselves. However, we know this isn't possible to do alone. There is no way we can work and survive while Nixon is going through a transplant.

Through social media, news about the fundraiser is spreading extremely fast. It is overwhelming to see the amount of people that want to help us. Two million dollars is too steep to collect from friends and family, especially as quickly as we need it. We need to be creative.

The next day, we post a message on social media to see if any of our friends and family knows anyone in the media, newspaper, or television. We want to bring attention to the fact that the insurance company is denying a child a chance at life. We figure people will pay attention, the insurance company will find out and maybe, to avoid negative publicity, just maybe, they will approve it. Again, so many insanely kind people are helping us. We contact all of the local news stations and newspapers in Chicago. A major newspaper responds first. They want to put Nixon's story on the front page of the Sunday paper. This is amazing! The newspaper reporter interviews us, and we tell them everything. She sends over the HIPAA forms for us to permit her to speak to our insurance company. The next day, we find out that the insurance approved anything transplant related for Nixon for one year. It's ridiculous that it requires news companies to get in touch with them for people to actually listen. I hate having to go that route, but you gotta do what you gotta do.

While preparing for the transplant, I start searching social media to find out who else has this disease. I find a Gaucher's Type 2 page that Ozzie and I both joined. As we look at this page, it seems like most of these families were also told to enjoy their children, and there isn't any hope. I have to post. They need to know that we found an option to take Nixon for a stem cell transplant. The replies I am receiving take me by surprise. I am shocked because many of these members are not fond of our idea. Based on the responses that we are getting from other parents, we delete our post and our profiles from that page.

Surprisingly, just a few days later Ozzie receives a private message from a woman who lives in Florida. She said she is proud of our decision. She and her husband also chose to do a transplant for their daughter. We know we need to speak with them, so I text to see if we can call her on the phone.

Later that night, we connect with the mom and dad and learn that their daughter was the only person, thus far, to go through the journey that we were about to take. Her daughter's transplant was a little different because the bone marrow was donated by a sibling. Nixon's bone marrow will come from donated umbilical cord blood. They shared with us that the roughest part of the transplant will be the chemotherapy. Then, they give us insight on the grueling process while waiting for the transplant to actually take. They continue with some lighthearted conversation to congratulate us on soon becoming "experts in waiting."

After the transplant, everything will be depleted in his system. Then each day, we will wait with the anticipation to see if the first red and white blood cell starts growing. Next is checking on the platelets to see if the transplant actually engrafted. Then, we have to hope that he doesn't get graft versus host disease. But this couple did it. They went through it, and their daughter survived it!

They are the only family that we have spoken with, so far, that gave us the drive and encouragement that we need. We need confirmation from someone who knows how this works and that it is only for Nixon's own good. They also explain why some of the people in the Gaucher's community do not agree with our decision. Some believe that we are extending the inevitable and dragging on such a horrible disease. They just want it to go away. But how the heck is it going to go away if you don't try to do something about it? Well, we found a family who had the courage and gave us the courage to do the same thing. They are excited for us, and they gave us additional hope.

This conversation is important for both of our families. We are no longer alone, anymore.

Before we head into this part of the journey, there is one other thing that Ozzie needs to get off of his chest. He called his liaison friend from the drug company and told her that we no longer need their money, nor their support. As I carefully overhear his conversation, he explains that we are starting to fully understand how and why doctors are promoting their drug, why hospitals have their pamphlets and brochures to hand out, and all geneticists are advocates for this drug therapy. It's because all of these people's pockets are lined with money at our child's expense. It is just mind-boggling how a drug company can make so much money from insurance companies and patients for a drug that doesn't even cure anything. She didn't say much.

The next call is to the doctors in Ohio to read them the riot act. He explains the results that Dr. Escolar shared, along with the transplant option. Then, they respond that they actually know of her. Well, why the heck didn't they tell us about her, then? Because when we were visiting them, they told us that if there was any option out there for this disease, they would know about it. Was this option not worth sharing? Apparently not. Everything is all starting to tie together. We are now starting to understand why the doctors in Ohio avoided telling us about Dr. Escolar. They made sure that we had every brochure and pamphlet they had about the drug company. It was all about money; all of it. It makes us so sick to our stomachs. People are what is most important. Not money, a job, a house, etc. People make the world go around.

We have one week until we leave for Pennsylvania. We call the non-profit organization connected to the hospital to reserve our living quarters. It is truly incredible that these resources are available now for families who go through what we are about to experience. Fortunately, we are released from of our apartment lease, and they are giving us a month to move everything out. Once again, generosity is overwhelming. My parents and their friends are volunteering to pack our things and move them to my parent's house after we leave. This gives us one less thing to worry about. All we need now is to start packing what we need for Pennsylvania. I didn't even care what we bring as long as Nixon has what he needs. Plus, even if we forget anything, my mom said she could ship it to us. At that point, I was on autopilot. What are we doing? Are we making the right decision? I know this is what we should do, but what if it doesn't work? His short life could be cut even shorter. But Ozzie and I decide that if we don't go through with this, we won't be able to live with ourselves wondering "what if." Miracles happen every day in medicine. He's going to survive this, and I'm not going to break down. I'm not going to fall apart. Not when there is still a chance. We are doing it!

It is a hot Friday in June, and I am finding the emotions come easily on my last day of work. I have to resign, but they will welcome me back whenever I am ready. I am sad to be leaving, but I am excited to start our journey to help save Nixon. I have been with these people every day for the past ten years. They are like my family. I literally have spent more time with them than anyone else in my life. Every single one of them attended our wedding, and they mean the world to me. Now, I'm going to be with a different group of people every day for the rest of the year; people who are doctors, nurses, and sick children. It will definitely be a change. Some of my customers sent me flowers and gifts. Towards the end of the day, my coworkers surprised me with gifts, my favorite lunch, deep dish pizza, and a cake that read:

N-    *Number One Fighter*
I-    *Incredible Mommy and Daddy*
X-    *Xtremely Courageous*
O-    *Onward Journey*
N-    *New Beginnings*

*Best Wishes!*

It feels very odd walking out the door, but I know this is what I need to do.

That night, my group of best friends invited me out for food, drinks, laughter and tears. They each gave me a hand-written letter to open on the days when I was feeling sad or couldn't handle what was going on. They wrote me a poem, and gave me a necklace that symbolized "Mighty." There was a card in it that said, "Your vision, spirit and passion make incredible things happen. Wear your necklace as a reminder that you can move mountains!" As I read it, I break down because I don't know how I am going to do this. How can I move mountains when I physically cannot do anything except sit and watch Nixon go through all of this? He is the love of my life, and if something happens to him, I will be lifeless. One of my best friends, Jamie, recently shared a quote she found,

> *"A spouse who loses their partner is a widow; a child who loses a parent is an orphan; but there is no word for a parent who loses a child because it is indescribable."*
> – JAY NEUGEBOREN

I never want to know that feeling, and my friends assured me that I was doing the right thing. I have to do this, and it is going to work.

As it is our last Saturday in Chicago, we spend the day packing the last of our belongings. The next morning, on Father's Day,

Ozzie will drive to Pennsylvania with his brother. On Monday, I will fly with my mom and Nixon. I can't believe it's time. We are leaving Chicago to move to Pennsylvania indefinitely, and we have no idea what the future is going to hold.

~

"Great things are done by a small series of small things brought together."

– Vincent Van Gogh

## Four

Week 1: Father's Day, June 15, 2014

I HAVE TO SAY that the "Father of the Year Award" definitely goes to my husband on Father's Day. In two weeks of flurry, he packed up our life and drove everything we owned to Pennsylvania on Father's Day. As if that wasn't enough, he didn't even get to spend his first Father's Day with his son. Amazing sacrifices made for a chance to save Nixon's life. This is the true meaning of a great dad. Late last night, Ozzie made it to the housing complex provided by the hospital. He unpacked the car and began to make a comfortable home for us. This morning, my mom, Nixon and I arrive. As I walk in through the front doors, I marvel at my surroundings. I can't believe how nice this place is for families to live while enduring such difficult experiences.

As I walk off the elevator, I notice a picture hanging on the wall. It reads,

> *"This is the house where families meet to continue their lives,*
> *to eat and sleep, to find their strengths, and dry their tears,*
> *to look forward with hope to better years. This is the house*
> *that becomes their home. This is the house that love built."*

I make a promise to myself to read that picture every day. I will draw strength from something so simple yet so touching. This "home away from home" has apartments for 60 families, and allows families to stay as long as we need. Prior to our arrival, in my mind, I pictured the space to be like a hotel room, but surprisingly, it is an actual one-bedroom apartment with a living room, bathroom, bedroom, and kitchen, which includes a refrigerator and microwave. It was quite cozy. Quite a gift.

If that wasn't enough, almost every day there are families and organizations that volunteer to cook breakfast, lunch and dinner for the families in residence. Another gift. It will be nice to have a home-cooked meal when possible. I've never been excited about hospital cafeteria food.

As we check in, I glance at some of the families walking in the halls, heading to the elevators. These people know what we are going through. Again, we are not alone. Yet, another gift.

During this first week while we are here, Nixon will begin the pre-transplant tests on Tuesday; luckily, these are all outpatient exams. With it being Monday, we take the day to organize our new apartment. We take a walk to familiarize ourselves with the surroundings. There are many shops, pizza places, and restaurants so close to each other that it reminds us of Chicago. The streets are so narrow and have many alleys, typical for an East Coast City. As I stand at the top of a hill, viewing the setting below me, I think about how this is going to be our new home, indefinitely.

Tuesday comes quickly and slowly at the same time. I have a feeling this will be our "new norm." During the clinic appointment, we meet Dr. Mark and the transplant team that will be working with us. In addition to Dr. Mark, there are 4 nurse practitioners, and 4 other BMT (bone marrow transplant) doctors that will rotate every few weeks. It is apparent that this group will be our family and friends for the coming months. They make us feel very comfortable and speak to us in terms that we understand. This is important and makes it easier for me to put my son's life in their hands. Five months is the minimum length of stay, and of those five, three will be in-patient care for Nixon. That's if everything goes okay. The following two months will be outpatient while residing at our new apartment connected to the hospital. I would rather be safe than sorry, and near instead of far, so this makes sense to me. Ozzie and I are good with it.

With long-term care, they want long-distance families to be as close as possible for as long as possible. They even asked us if we would be willing to move to Pennsylvania! Being that today was only our third day here, I needed more time to consider that idea.

Dr. Mark and his team covered the entire process and protocol with us, including what our days will most likely consist of. The part I am most scared about is the chemotherapy. He is going to get mouth sores. In addition, there will come a time period where we will have to bathe him five times a day because if he sweats; the chemo can burn his skin. He will also lose all of his beautiful dark brown hair and long luscious eyelashes. But I know they will eventually grow back.

They explain that the most difficult part will be a couple of days before the transplant and about a month after the transplant. Before is difficult because he will get the strongest boost of chemo along with the worst side effects. A month after is painful because the cells are starting to grow which causes bone pain and mucositis which feels like heartburn from your throat all the way to your gut. The month after is also the most critical because that determines if the transplant actually takes. My heart is just broken for him. He has been poked with needles so many times that three of his veins already popped. They are running out of spots from where to draw blood. My poor little pin cushion! After meeting with Dr. Mark's team, Nixon heads down the hall for a brief evaluation, a blood draw, and has a nasal swab to test for infections. He also had a chest x-ray and an "ECHO" test to check his heart function. Luckily everything came back normal.

Wednesday is a much more involved day with many tests and evaluations. First is the GFR test for kidney function. Next, the CT scanned his head, chest, abdomen, and pelvis. He looks so cute sucking on his pacifier tucked all snug in the CT scanner. The scanner is even themed like a pirate ship. A little bit of amusement doesn't hurt. Once again, everything came back normal other than his spleen and liver were enlarged, which the disease caused. It wasn't a surprise, as we already knew it. Now that the testing is completed, we are full steam ahead with the transplant. They found three matches for him; two from the East coast and one from the West coast. A rating of 6/6 is the ideal match for a transplant. His matches were all 4/6. They are still able to perform a transplant with this ranking. They said it was harder to find a match for him than they expected.

The next step is to test which cord blood out of the three donors is the best match. It's interesting; I didn't realize that about every two weeks, they perform transplants on storage disorders at this hospital; which is more common than I thought. I'm starting to like the team here as well. I am definitely getting good vibes from the doctors who are taking care of him. As scary as all of this is, I just need to take things one day at a time.

Today is Thursday and marks Nixon's enzyme replacement therapy day. This will continue throughout the transplant process to help shrink his spleen and liver and will end the procedures for this week. Starting Monday, the real adventure begins. He will be admitted to the hospital to begin the transplant process. He will get catheters put into his heart, and they will start him on a liquid version of chemotherapy. I am very concerned with the side effects, but the doctors assure me that they know how to treat all side effects. The real problem will be if he rejects the transplant because then his bone marrow will grow back, which means he will still have the disease. But that is not going to happen; I have to believe that it's not.

With some free time ahead of us, we want to enjoy the weekend. Tour Time! We head to the zoo; one of our favorite places back home. It actually reminds me of our favorite zoo back home as it has the aquarium, some historical sites, restaurants and shops. It's a beautiful summer day, but a little too hot for comfort. At the end of the day, we take Nixon for his first bar experience. Don't worry, alcohol wasn't served, but we watched the USA win their first world cup soccer game! As a seven-month-old, he was as ecstatic as he could be. Go USA!

As the weekend ends, a part of me can't help but think about how our life has come to this moment. How does it change in an instant? It's really surreal. To help calm my nerves, I talked myself into believing that we are on a vacation this week. The free weekend of fun definitely helps with that. However, I can't seem to escape it, and I feel so naïve. In the back of my mind, probably like most of us, I always knew about unfortunate circumstances in this world; that kids get sick; and hardships happen out of nowhere. But I guess I never truly realized how many people are enduring such serious circumstances. Here, at one hospital in the world, we are surrounded by so many sick children. Everywhere I look, every corner I turn, whether it is walking near the cafeteria or even going to do laundry, I see a child who is sick. It breaks my heart every day. I have no idea how I will stay strong through this.

Before I fall asleep at the end of our fun weekend, I hear a helicopter land on the roof; a helicopter that I hear frequently throughout the day. That helicopter carries organs and transports sick children to this hospital, even from other states. We are at a hospital where transplants are a common everyday occurrence. The best doctors who are specialists in pediatric transplants, storage disorders and other illnesses are here, in this place, doing everything they can each and every day to save children. Hearing that helicopter gives me comfort in knowing that a child's life is about to be saved. That night, the sound of the helicopter and the meaning of its presence helps me drift off into a deep sleep thinking of how lucky we are to live in a place where things like this are possible.

**Week 2: June 22, 2014**

While other families are outside enjoying the June weather at parks, play dates and picnics, our Monday morning begins with Nixon's first surgery to place two broviac central lines into his heart. These lines will be used throughout the transplant process to administer medicine and draw blood very easily without him getting poked so much. The central lines are long, hollow tubes made of soft rubber-like material with an opening called a lumen. Each line will be inserted into the large vein leading directly into the heart.

My seven-month-old son is having surgery. Surgery! While in the waiting room for about 30 minutes, my nerves get the best of me. I want to vomit and cry, but instead I head to our temporary apartment and pour a glass of wine. I open and read one of the letters my friends sent, as I sip... gulp down my wine. It indeed helps me, and I feel a sense of calm, if only for a short time.

After I feel a little more composed, I walk back to meet Ozzie in the surgical waiting area filled with of many anxious and worried parents just like me. Parents whose legs can't stop shaking, who have the look of worry splattered all over their faces, and who keep pacing back and forth. I start a conversation with a lady who is waiting for her son to come out of his surgery. We share our stories with each other, trying to make it lighthearted and help time pass. We even become friends on a popular social media site. Then my mind wanders, and I start thinking about how teeny Nixon is and how will they get everything in its proper place within Nixon's little body? Well… they didn't get everything in properly. His surgery finished after three hours. While in recovery, they snap a chest x-ray. They find the central line flipped where it shouldn't be in his chest. They head back to surgery and replace it. Two surgeries in one day. This is the longest seven hours of my life.

By the evening, we finally make it up to the transplant floor, 9B (9th Floor, B Wing). I look around at all of the nurses who are hard at work. They are all so pretty and appear very nice and friendly. Some remind me of my friends at home. Gosh, I do miss them. I miss having our girls' nights, seeing their kids, talking about what happens throughout the week, and having monthly dinners at our favorite wine restaurant. But then I snap back to my new reality; we will have those nights once again, when we get through this battle.

We arrive in his room, and Nixon starts to have trouble breathing. He is literally gasping for air. Suddenly, about 20 doctors and nurses flood into the room. Ozzie stays by Nixon, and I am paralyzed standing in the corner with tears in my eyes. Fear takes over my body, as I wonder if we made the right decision. One of the nurses walks over to give me a hug and hold my hand. A respiratory therapist is called to come to his room. She is responsible for keeping his lungs clean, infection free and the airway open. She gives him a few breathing treatments until he is stable and resting comfortably. It's hard to believe only 30 minutes have passed as it feels like a lifetime. Two surgeries in one day and being intubated two times can sometimes cause breathing issues. Other than that, central line placements are a piece of cake. If this is how our first day starts, then I have no idea what I'm in for.

Tuesday comes and marks his first blood transfusion because his red blood cell count is too low. This is not normal. When his hemoglobin gets too low, it causes him to feel sluggish and look pale. After receiving a rich, red colored bag of blood, the transfusion adjusted his levels where needed. Color flowed back into his cute little cheeks. Ahhhh. I can breathe again. Luckily that's all we had to deal with today. After Nixon's breathing trouble yesterday, I don't know how much more I can handle.

Chemotherapy begins. His first round is a low dose as a test run to make sure my baby boy can handle it. The chemo is administered through an IV bag for about 4 hours, and its job is to wipe out his white blood cells. At this point, our luck strikes again. Lo and behold, he has an allergic reaction to the chemotherapy. However, the doctors assure us that this is common. The antidote is to give acetaminophen and an antihistamine whenever he needs a transfusion.

As the day progresses and the chemo is completed, he spikes a 102-degree fever! Never a dull moment, I tell ya. By Thursday, they give him a higher dose of the same type of chemo, but this one requires a 7 hour drip. This experience brings on another fever and hives pop up all over his body. This is all starting to scare me. We have only been here for two weeks, and it's been one thing after another. I keep asking the doctors "If this was your child, would you be doing this?" They keep saying, "Yes." Everything that was not supposed to happen has happened so far. It is becoming a nightmare. I am starting to get apprehensive, but I know if I tell them to stop this whole thing, then Nixon will, for sure, die. It's just terrifying; I hate seeing him like this. I express my concerns to Dr. Mark, and he explains, "it will be like a roller coaster with the good and bad, but keep telling yourself that the end will be good. It has to get really bad before it gets really good." He said, "You will continue to feel like you want to stop this whole thing until everything starts to continue to go uphill." Words that I need to remember.

This Saturday and Sunday in the hospital are his "rest days." However, he is already experiencing the effects of the chemo and is feeling crappy. Luckily, we are having some moments throughout the day where he smiles and even laughs. This kid has the biggest smile that just makes you melt, and his laugh just gives you butterflies.

We are even able to leave his room with him for a few hours. His white blood cell count is now less than 300, which is what is supposed to happen within the first week. A normal range for white cells is between 5,000-10,000. The chemo worked! The goal is to get them to zero by transplant day.

Throughout the week, he is also taking a liquid version of chemo that he receives through a syringe. Each day, he still drinks his 30 ounces of formula. This makes his mama happy! Overall, for the first week as an in-patient, Nixon seems to be handling everything quite well, even with all the complications. He still seems strong and is ready to continue this fight.

By the end of Sunday, Ozzie and I were letting our nerves get the best of us. This is hard, a lot harder than I thought it would be, and it is just the beginning. We literally just sit in a room together with Nixon all day long, sleeping there, eating there and just watching him. We are helpless. There is nothing we can do except hold his hand through this. I ended up going to the store earlier in the day to just get out for a bit. I picked up some soft, comfy blankets that "feel like puppies," as Ozzie put it and other items to make the hospital room feel a little more like home. I needed to surround myself with happy things. Every night, much to Ozzie's dismay, I fell asleep to reruns of my favorite sitcoms about friends or happy, funny families. No drama, no scary TV, just plain old sitcoms. When Nix sleeps, I take breaks just to get out of the room. I walked up and down the transplant floor. I see the kids going through the same thing as Nixon and parents who feel the same as Ozzie and me. I am scared to talk to them though; I don't want to know what to expect; not yet. I start to make small talk with some of the nurses. I can't imagine having a job where you see families go through this day in and day out. But they are someone for us to talk to, other than each other. Even though I have my brave face on, I know they can smell my fear from a mile away.

**10 days till "Transplant Day" a.k.a. "T-Day" (July 9th)**

**Week 3: June 29, 2014**

As June comes to a close, the hot days of summer are upon us. Nixon is now scheduled to have chemotherapy every single day this week. It is a mild chemo that stops cell growth and causes the cells to die. Fortunately, it is only about an hour each day through the IV bag. We thought he would be able to get a pass to leave his room on Monday, but his white cells were too low. They give patients passes so they get a chance to leave the room, take a walk through the hospital, go outside in the "healing garden," or even go back to their apartments. The good thing is that because his counts are low, it means the chemo is working. The bad news is since his last day to leave the room is today, he is stuck in there for a good three months now. Looking on the bright side, he is happy and loves when we make duck sounds! It's his new thing. We are trying to keep him as happy as possible because I keep hearing a little girl screaming in pain in the room down the hall from us. She recently had her transplant. When the cells start to attach onto your bone marrow, it's very painful. This is something that I'm not looking forward to. AT ALL. My heart just aches every time I hear her. I don't know how I'm going to get through this, I really don't. So for now, I'm just going to keep quacking.

Tuesday and Wednesday came and went with few sessions of physical therapy, occupational therapy and speech therapy. He is sitting up better than he ever was, not quite on his own yet, but he is getting there. As far as eating, he LOVES his bottle and he hates baby food with a passion. He hates carrots, bananas and any type of solids that we put in his mouth. I decide to hold off and try when he starts to feel better. He has been handling his chemo like a champ, and it doesn't seem to be as bad as we expected! The doctors are very pleased with how he is doing, and we are on track with his transplant for July 9th.

As our second weekend of in-patient care approaches, Nixon starts a stronger version of chemo. This is the chemo that will cause him to lose his hair. It will also make the space in the bone marrow for the new cells to grow, as well as fully knocking out his immune system. Side effects are hair loss (which is already starting to thin out) and getting mucositis. This is as bad as it sounds. It's a condition that will feel like he has sunburn from the top of his throat to his bottom area. He will get mouth sores and slimy mucus. His skin will change color, so that he will look like he has been at the beach! And he will be nauseous. We also have to bathe him 3-5 times a day because if he sweats, the chemo can burn him.

As we are settled in the hospital for the weekend, he starts to scream in pain. He is choking on the mucus, and it seems like the nausea is kicking in because he will not eat. I start to feel devastated, but he still has his moments throughout the day where he smiles and laughs from time to time.

We are at the beginning of the worst part, which will last about three weeks. A very scared feeling is starting to take over inside of me. My fear is that the transplant won't take, meaning his cells will start to grow back instead of the donor's, which can happen. However, Dr. Mark said that in the two years he has been at this hospital he has not seen that happen yet. I'm also worrying about graft versus host disease, which is when the regular blood cells start to fight the new cord blood cells. I know I shouldn't think this way, but I am his mom, and he is the person who I love most in this world. I can't help it. I'm terrified, and I feel like I'm going to fall apart. I have to prepare for the worst and hope for the best. The sooner the hard part happens the closer we are to this being over. As I walk back to the apartment for my daily shower, I start thinking that it really isn't fair that this little human being has to go through something so horrific.

My parents visited this week, and it couldn't have been better timing. Having to watch my baby go through chemo is not easy. It is 4th of July this week, and we can take Nixon to the corner room of the floor and watch fireworks out the window. But Oz and I both need a break. The only time we ever leave his hospital room is to shower, to get food, or to take a walk. We went to pick up some groceries, had a drink together and just talked about how this was not the life that we mapped out for ourselves. But while we were gone, we couldn't get back there fast enough. I want to be with him every second. I want to switch places with him. I wish it was me and not him.

3 days till T-Day...

Week 4: July 6, 2014

This is it. Transplant week! It's Monday, and Nixon is receiving the heaviest dose of chemo, yet. This is the final dose of chemo he will ever need, and of course, he is handling it very well. Today he stopped eating because of the mucositis. He has sores and a bunch of buildup in his mouth that looks like slime. This is brutal. He also has started to throw up stomach lining, and he screams in pain to the point to where he turns blue and then chokes on his saliva.

They gave him some lorazepam last night to calm his stomach from nausea. I remember that the family in Florida told us that it would be our best friend through this whole process. I just kept holding him and telling him how sorry I was. Tuesday is supposed to be a "rest day" before the transplant, but instead, he receives one medication after another to prepare him for the big day. He is still smiling and playing, but you can clearly tell that the days of chemo are really starting to take a toll on him. Tomorrow will be a new beginning. He will receive his new stem cells and will be starting over. I feel like it is the night I went into labor because the next day I brought a new life into this world.

**Transplant Day. Wednesday, July 9, 2014**

The day starts with Nixon getting pre-medicated. Then, his nurse brings in what looks like a bag of blood, but it isn't blood; it is the stem cells; these were the best match that they could find. That bag is the most important thing in my world at this moment. That bag is the possibility of my son's chance at this life. I can't keep my eyes off it.

In preparation, the nurses double and triple check Nixon's social security number, birthdate, blood type, blood type of the donor, etc. It seems really serious, and I am glad that they take it so seriously. The cord blood is run over about one-hour into his broviac central line. The nurse stays in the room the entire time to watch him, and Dr. Mark keeps peeking his head in every fifteen minutes to make sure all is okay. Ozzie takes out the video camera as we feel it is something that we need to remember. I know one thing that I will remember is creamed corn. The entire room smells like creamed corn, and we were told that every time a transplant happens that is the smell. Not sure why or how, but it is. Besides having a little fussiness, Nix breezes through the transplant process. No fever or high blood pressure. He did great! After it was over, he rests comfortably. I'm still completely baffled and in shock that my son just had a stem cell transplant today. It seems surreal, but that's it! All of this for one little bag that takes one hour!? What a breeze! This,

I can handle.

Ha! I spoke too soon. From that day on, the mucositis started kicking in hard core. Every time he has a bowel movement, he screams in excruciating pain. The slimy mucus causes him to choke pretty frequently, which requires us to suction it from his throat. We are learning to become nurses ourselves. So far, he needed two platelet transfusions and one blood transfusion. It can be dangerous for his platelets to get too low, as they help cause the blood to clot. It is normal to have transfusions after a transplant, but it usually doesn't happen until after day +6. We are only on day +4. Since he stopped eating, he gets his nutrition through an IV bag, and they put him on morphine every three hours to help with the pain that is caused from the transplant. It is an extremely agonizing process as the stem cells find their place in his body and start to grow. We start to deal with pain management, but the worst part of the mucositis is usually not until around day +10 which is July 14.

Saturday isn't seeming to be a very good day. Nix is in a lot of pain, and the mucositis is bad. He just looks so sad all of the time now, and I feel tormented. We are in the worst situation, and the worst of the worst is still to come. When he's not screaming in pain, he sleeps.

Sunday is the first day that Nixon seems somewhat back to his normal self. He is more alert, smiling and even playing with his toys. But now begins the waiting process to identify if he is engrafted. Engrafted means that the new stem cells have taken over his body and this usually happens around day +21, but it can sometimes happen sooner.

Some people think that a stem cell transplant is an actual surgery. I thought the same thing. I was baffled when I came to find out the actual process. Apparently, that is the easy part; it's all of the stuff before and after that is the hard part. Since everybody is different, the doctors have a baseline on what to expect, but it's difficult to predict because each person reacts differently.

At this point, we continue to take everything one day at a time. But now we have to wait, and I have a very hard time being patient. I keep telling myself over and over, "good things come to those who wait."

So, while I'm waiting, I find distractions on social media and TV. I scroll through the posts, and I read everything that everyone else is doing. It sucks that we have to be here. It makes me sad, angry and jealous. But when I look at my son's face, I know that I would do this over a thousand more times if I had to, to make him better. I'm starting to get scared about what he may or may not be able to do when this is all over. I have a fear that he may not walk. I know that I won't know until everything is all said and done, but it's hard to not think about it all. I'm just hoping and praying that things turn out as best as they possibly can, and he can have the best life possible. But that fear just sits inside of me, waiting, haunting. However, I know that no matter what happens, as long as he smiles every day, that will be enough for me.

~

"I love the man that can smile in trouble, that can gather strength from distress, and grow brave by reflection. 'Tis the business of little minds to shrink, but he whose heart is firm, and whose conscience approves his conduct, will pursue his principles unto death."

– Thomas Paine

# Five

**Week 5: July 13, 2014**

To START THE WEEK, Nixon seems to be holding his own. The doctors are very pleased with how he is doing. However, he has needed transfusions almost every day because his spleen keeps eating his platelets. Gaucher's is a storage disease, which causes the liver and spleen to store cells, such as platelets. Even putting that aside, platelet transfusions are a normal routine after a child has had a transplant. The body takes time to adjust to making its own, since the immune system is depleted.

On Thursday, he received his enzyme replacement therapy to help reduce the size of his liver and spleen. This will prevent the organs from eating his platelets. The past couple of nights, he has been getting oxygen while he sleeps. His breathing is very shallow due to the lack of room that he has in his small little body from his enlarged organs. He is also still on a continuous morphine drip for his pain from the mucositis.

I will never forget this Friday morning. It is this day that my full head of hair baby became bald. Before today, like when he was born, Nixon had a beautiful head of dark brown hair. This morning, he woke up with a mohawk. Every piece of hair on his sides and back had fallen out from sleeping on it. All that was left was the hair on the top of his head. When Ozzie brushed his fingers through what remained, it fell out into his hand. He thought it was the coolest thing. While I was out of the room he decided to make my baby completely bald by gently pulling it out with his hand. I couldn't believe it because he looked so cute with his mohawk. I put some of it in a plastic bag and kept it.

His white blood cell count is still under 300. Once his numbers are over 500 for three consecutive days, then he is considered engrafted. After a few days of engraftment, they test to find the percentage of donor blood in his system. He has been doing physical therapy, but still cannot sit up yet. He needs to get more head control and isn't able to tilt it down. His liver and spleen are so enlarged that it makes him uncomfortable. He looks like humpty dumpty because he just bobbles back and forth. But he's so stinking cute! They are hopeful that once his enlarged organs start shrinking then he should be on track to sit up again. We have tried giving him his bottle. He looks interested and grabs for it, but then once it gets to his mouth, he no longer wants it. He still has the mucositis. Hopefully, as that clears, he will want to eat again. The mucositis won't clear until he starts producing some white blood cells. We pray every day that sooner rather than later, the doctor will come in and tell us that he finally has some counts. As they say quite frequently around here "GROW CELLS GROW!!!"

**Week 6: July 20, 2014**

The late July days have been quite warm here, but it feels good to get outside and have the sun beaming on my face a few times a day. On Monday, Nixon didn't seem to be himself. Although, what was "himself" nowadays? I had a terrible feeling inside of me that something was wrong.

It's now Tuesday morning, and he is having trouble breathing. They did a chest x-ray, and his broviac line in his heart flipped again. The good thing (if there is a good thing) is that it flipped into a central blood vessel that still goes to his heart. Who knows when it happened, as they have given him so many medications through that line that even the smallest of pushes could have caused it to flip. He can't have surgery to fix it because he has no blood cell counts still. They also found a break in his line that they tried to fix, but it didn't work. We hope that open air did not enter through the hole in that break; otherwise, it could lead to an infection, directly into his heart. Since he has four broviac lines, they can still administer medicine with the other three. It's just not the doctors' preferred route. They are running some tests to rule out infection. Unfortunately, he does have fluid in his lungs, so they are going to try to "dry him out" with a diuretic and see if that helps. He has been on oxygen, which is helping, but he is still not breathing effortlessly like he should. So, the doctors ordered him to transfer to the PICU floor (Pediatric Intensive Care Unit). My heart sunk into my stomach. We were just getting used to the transplant floor. Now, we are going to be in a completely new environment with new people that I don't know. Something was telling me that I wasn't going to like this.

The rest of the week will be spent monitoring his lungs. He has gained a ton of weight, but it is all fluid, which isn't a good thing. One day his lungs are clear; the next day they aren't. He is on a high flow oxygen tank to help him breathe, which he pulls out of his nose every chance he gets; tape and all. His breathing has not changed much, and he cannot be released from PICU until it does. Watching your child having trouble breathing is heart wrenching. I wish that I could breathe for him. The doctors believe that his breathing is attributed to the fluid in his lungs as well as the start of engraftment. He does have some white blood cells, but they keep rising and falling. This is expected.

This week continues to be a challenge. Two of his four central lines clotted now, and they lost access. The other two kept stopping and starting. Some of his medicines are sticky. If you don't use the same tubes for the same medicine, the tubes harden if the medicine doesn't continuously run through them. This happens sometimes, and it isn't good because he still has weeks where those lines are needed.

Towards the end of the week, they stopped his lipids (food by fluids) because of the limited access to his broviac lines. They also don't want him to get an overload of more fluid. To get more ports, they put IV's in his arm and his foot. By Sunday morning, they lost the foot access because it gave out when his vein collapsed. They are worried about doing surgery to replace his broviac central lines because of his breathing. Since he is on high flow oxygen, it's too risky to put him under anesthesia. On top of all of this, he has not had a bowel movement for four days. This is a big concern, as he screams in pain about every twenty minutes due to discomfort, yet no one can pinpoint the cause of his discomfort. At this point, we are at a standstill as they try to figure out how to address all of these issues as best as they can. Until they get everything under control, he will continue to be in PICU.

The transplant floor has colorful walls, and the halls are filled with upbeat people. Disney characters and sports players regularly visit, and they provide our children with as much of a home life atmosphere as possible. On the contrary, the PICU is a completely different world. The walls are plain; there is limited access from visitors; the mood is dark; the kids are sicker; and the families are more scared. All you hear is the beeping sound of monitors and alarms. The best analogy to describe this space is from a popular TV series. 9B is like being in jail, but PICU is like being in the SHU (Security Housing Unit, also known as solitary confinement). Quite a few times, we overheard some of the nurses getting phone calls about kids who were getting airlifted to this hospital. We even overheard a phone call about a child who ended up drinking liquid drain cleaner. Each person in each room of this floor has a different story. If only walls could talk. A few of our nurses have been wonderful. They sit outside of Nixon's room constantly monitoring him. They are friendly and have been taking great care of him. They help give us comfort so we aren't scared. It takes a very big person with a very big heart to work down here. I give them a ton of credit.

Nixon seems like he is mad at the world, and he should be with everything he has to go through. He hates his oxygen tubes in his nose and keeps trying to take them out. He is sleeping a lot, but he also gets woken up a lot because they are constantly checking his vitals. I know vitals are important, but sleep is also important for a baby. I saw one of the nurse practitioners from Dr. Mark's team, and she said that the extra fluid is more than likely due to the engrafting. They also saw some white blood cells under the microscope! Not enough to be over 300, which is what we need, but they are there and starting to work. Finally, a little bit of good news!

### Week 7: July 27, 2014

It is already the end of July. Summer seems to be flying by without us. This week started out with getting Nixon's pain under control. Every 20-30 minutes, he wails back and forth and screams like the exorcist. It is heart breaking. He was on a continuous morphine drip, but the doctors switched him over to a continuous dilaudid drip which made a world of a difference. Both are pain relieving drugs but dilaudid is three to four times stronger. He is now in a comfortable state. The transplant causes bone pain and itching which can be very uncomfortable, especially for a little one. But we realized that the reason for this was his cells were finally growing!

Tuesday was glorious! It was the first day that his numbers for the ANC, Absolute Neutrophil Count, were over 500. The ANC is the most important number to monitor after a transplant. Nixon's white cell count was 1100, and his ANC was 760. One day down, two more to go before we can say he is engrafted!

Wednesday morning couldn't come quick enough. Ozzie and I were on the edge of our seats wanting to know his numbers. We woke up, grabbed our coffee and BOOM, the nurse came running in his room. He is above 500!

Thursday morning, we woke up like two children on Christmas morning. The nurse came in and read us his numbers. "NIXON IS OFFICALLY ENGRAFTED!" This means that the transplant is officially in his bone marrow. They will also start slowly weaning him off the oxygen. By Saturday night, he was officially breathing on his own. He actually pulled the tubes out of his nose and off of his face and started waving them in the air. I guess he knew he didn't need the oxygen anymore. He is now one step closer to leaving PICU. What a difference a week makes!

When you see your child in pain, you want nothing more than to experience that pain for them. When Nix was a baby, I was hesitant to even give him acetaminophen. We are now living in a world where natural and organic are becoming the norm. When we were home, I always tried natural remedies anytime he would cry. But after seeing him in the pain that he was in, I was willing to let these doctors give him anything they could to help him. Dilaudid was the answer at that time, and considering what Nixon had just been through, I let the natural remedies go out the window. His comfort was all that mattered. When we heard the amazing news that Nixon was officially engrafted, we felt an unimaginable sigh of relief. We are done with half of the battle. Now, we just need the new bone marrow to take over his body, stay, and make sure none of his old cells are left. This is called a chimerism test that measures the percentage of donor cells, which they will run in a few days when his engraftment is more stable. Have I mentioned that I hate waiting?

**Week 8: August 3, 2014**

Nixon's breathing is finally under control to the point where they feel he is stable enough to have surgery. Late Monday night, he had surgery to replace his four central broviac lines. Before he went into surgery, he laughed and smiled for the first time in 28 days. I felt like butterflies were fluttering in my stomach, and it was the best feeling to have before he went into surgery. It felt amazing. He was a champ, and everything went as good as it could have. During the surgery, he had to be intubated, which is when they insert a tube down his throat to help him breathe. The surgeon replaced all his lines, and they now work beautifully. Once again, after surgery, he needed some breathing treatments from the respiratory team. Like the previous time, they were able to get his breathing back under control.

On Tuesday, after a night of recovery, he was well enough to be released from PICU to 9B. I could not believe it because I was so sure that we would be there until next week. The following few days he started to become his normal self. He was smiling and laughing again and playing with his toys. He recognized his favorite nurses who came to visit. When he saw them, he would get a huge smile on his face and flutter his eyebrows up and down like he was flirting with them. They got a kick out of him.

On Friday, as we were sitting in our room, four doctors came in at the same time. It scared the hell out of me because Dr. Mark was with them, and I had no idea what they were about to say. They could see the fear written all over my face. I was about to crap myself. But Dr. Mark just smiled and said, "Hey guess what? His chimerism test came back and Nixon is 100% DONOR!"

I literally just couldn't contain myself. I started screaming and crying, hugged every doctor in the room, and grabbed my phone and texted everyone that I knew. When you are in a situation like this, news like that is like winning the lottery. This means that the transplant worked! I couldn't believe it until they showed it to me in black and white. Sometimes, there is a chance that the test could come back with a majority of his cells as donor and some of his old cells could still be in his bone marrow. If this was the case, they would give him a boost with the 5% of the cord blood that they put on reserve. But he was fortunate enough that ALL 100% of his blood was the donor's, which is the best-case scenario!

When he is 100% donor blood, it means that he will no longer produce Gaucher cells. However, it does not mean that they are completely gone. He still has the previous cells that remain, BUT they will no longer continue to grow. For six months, he may still be affected from these cells, and we have no idea how it will affect him. We just have to hope and pray that he will continue to thrive until the Gaucher cells are completely gone. The doctors explained that they will run a test this week to be sure he is producing the enzyme he wasn't able to produce. We will continue to remain in the hospital until they can wean him off of his medicines and he starts to eat on his own. At that point, we will be able to move back to the apartment with him. Afterwards, we then start out-patient clinics and therapy which will most likely last until December. And then, we can go home. Gosh, do I miss home.

At the end of this week, I reflected on all that has happened. It's hard to believe everything that we have accomplished in the two months that we have been here. I can't even tell you the amount of courage that this little boy has had throughout this experience. I can do my best to describe what he has gone through, but having to physically see it day in and day out during this process, is beyond heartbreaking. The strength that this tiny human has is more than admirable. He has shown us that life is worth fighting for. Now, we must get him stronger every day so we can show him everything that this life has to offer.

~

"To enjoy good health, to bring true happiness to one's family, to bring peace to all, one must first discipline and control one's own mind. If a man can control his mind he can find the way to Enlightenment, and all wisdom and virtue will naturally come to him."

– Buddha

# Six

**Week 9: August 10, 2014**

This is what you call the dog days of August, and Sunday night was a long night for us. Nix was throwing up. It was really scary because he has not done that before, and I was actually by myself with him when it happened. I know that throwing up is not that big of a deal, but when you see your child do it for the first time it throws you for a loop. Nixon is our first child, and we are experiencing a lot of our parenting firsts while being in the hospital. We are always worried that all of these "firsts" are transplant related.

When Ozzie returns to the room, we notice a pool of blood on the floor. One of Nixon's lines was disconnected. It happened to be a line that was clotted. When they connected it, both lines on the right side stopped working. I was so scared and pissed because he just had surgery to get all of this fixed. They put a solution called TPA in the lines, which breaks up the clots. Two hours later they started working again.

We then learned why he has been getting sick. They are weaning him off the pain medicine that he was on in PICU. He is actually starting to have withdrawals! My baby who is nine-months-old is having withdrawals. He gets all clammy, rolls back and forth from one side to another and then throws up. Aside from when he has these episodes, he has been smiling and laughing uncontrollably. It is the best sound that I can hear. It steals my heart when he does that.

By Tuesday of this week, my parents came in to town for a visit and to give Ozzie and me a little break. A date is much needed for our relationship. This process is really hard on a marriage, but we are trying to stay as strong as possible and focus on Nixon. My parents must have been good luck charms because we also found out that Nix is making his own red blood cells already, and his hair is starting to grow back! Little things like this just make my day. I just keep praying that things continue to go where we need them. That night, the doctors said they were going to start taking him off the medicine that boosts his bone marrow to see if his counts continue to go up on their own. Gosh, I hope this kid can hold his own without the help of his meds. If he does, then it's just another step in the right direction.

They have a child life program on our floor to help make the children comfortable and give them things to do. The coordinator gave us a booklet called his "Daily Bead Journal" that we fill out every day. For every procedure, Nixon receives a bead and those beads then become a necklace. Some of the categories are chemotherapy, hair loss, being an inpatient, stem cell harvest such as TPN, IV nutrition, CT Scans, X-rays, transfusions, stem cell transplant, and the list goes on. Nixon's book was starting to get filled, and I didn't know if it was a good thing or a bad thing. I just knew that one day he can look at this and hopefully say "Wow... look at everything that I went through."

By the middle of the week, Nixon spiked a fever and developed a rash. He received his platelets, so it might have been a reaction. They cultured his central lines to check for infection and snapped a chest x-ray because his breathing was abnormal. They gave him acetaminophen and the anti-histamine, which worked. Later that afternoon, the fever and hives dissipated, and his x-ray was negative for pneumonia. I needed that news because it made it a lot easier for Ozzie and me to take a break and go on our date. A glass of wine was needed immediately. We ate at a restaurant near the football stadium, and then we walked around the downtown area. We saw quite a bit of the city and realized its beauty. It is similar to Chicago, and for a short minute, a part of me felt like I was back at home.

This week is proving to teach us that the transplant process is like the cha-cha. You take two steps forward and one step back. At the beginning of the week, we discovered that Nix is producing his own red blood cells! At the end of this same week, we found out that he developed antibodies that are attacking the red blood cells that he is making on his own! To hopefully kill the antibodies and maintain a positive cell count, they will administer a one-time, six-hour IV treatment that will hopefully help kill these antibodies and keep up his cell count. We should know in about a week or so if it worked.

While I was nervous with worry about his red blood cell issue, we received the most amazing news, ever. Nixon's body is now making the enzyme, glucocerebrocidaise!! Earlier, I explained that the white blood cells he produces were lacking this enzyme. White blood cells are supposed to be able to pass the blood brain barrier. This enzyme was not able to reach his brain, which causes his liver and spleen to become enlarged. They tested his donor white blood cells, and they are indeed making the enzyme that his white blood cells could not. Now, there is no reason to believe that it is not getting to his brain! No more enzyme replacement therapy! The fact that they are actually able to make something like this happen is crazy. We live in an amazing world!

This week, it hit Ozzie and me that our son is going to LIVE!!! Three months ago, there was no way it was even possible. Right now, Nixon has all of the blood, bone marrow, and stem cells that a normal child should have. Granted, we do not know how the remaining Gaucher cells will affect him because the doctors said it will take about six months before they leave him, but right now there is good reason to believe that he will live well past the age of three, unlike what we were originally told; and he could possibly have a full life. We are thankful to those original doctors, insurance companies, and Gaucher experts who doubted our son because they helped guide us to be stronger parents. Nixon just proved them wrong!

**Week 10: August 17, 2014**

As we approach the end of August, everything is going fabulous. Nixon's body is responding the way that it should and as well as it can. One of the doctors that is the head of the transplant team came to check on him and said, "He is a little tiger that will turn into a jaguar!" "Damn right," I thought. We begin to see major changes, and his beautiful head of hair just keeps on growing! The beginning of this week looked bright, and then lo and behold, by mid-week he had some issues with his breathing. He couldn't hold his stats, which means his breathing and heart rate kept going very low. On Tuesday, the ENT (ear, nose and throat) doctors ran a scope in through his nose and down his throat to see if there were any concerns. His trachea and airway looked great, so that was very reassuring. His pulmonary test showed "asthma like" signs, so they are giving him three breathing treatments each day and starting him on an inhaler. Although it was a scary two days, by Thursday, he no longer needed the breathing treatment. However, he will need the inhaler for a while.

Our current battle is trying to get Nixon to eat. Everyone warned us that it is a lengthy process and to be patient (There is that word again!). He does not want the bottle. Thankfully, on Saturday, he ate twelve spoonfuls of apple baby food, and he ate twenty spoonfuls of pears on Sunday! Finally, he is eating solid food. That new mom instinct inside of me has a very strong desire to make sure my child is fed well, even if he is getting what he needs through an IV. Towards the end of the week, while I was feeding him, I noticed something inside of his mouth. He popped his first tooth!! This is a great sign because we learned that growing teeth is part of the neurological process.

The doctors are pleased with Nixon's progress, and he is getting closer to being discharged as an outpatient. The nurses have started teaching Ozzie and me to change the dressing on his central lines and administer medicines through the lines. When we leave the hospital and return to our apartment, we will be in charge of all of this. It's scary because we must be so cautious to prevent the chance of passing germs that can lead to an infection which will go directly to his heart. I am very apprehensive about it, so for the nurses, I did it once, just to show them that I am capable, if needed. But, I have a feeling that Ozzie will be doing most of this. I now have a reason to call him Dr. Oz!

### Week 11: August 24, 2014

Finally, Nixon's stem cell transplant numbers are getting where we need them. They are slowly weaning him off of his IV medicines and switching to more oral medicines. He has slowly accepted his oral medicine and is even getting better with the bottle. I really want to avoid the gastrostomy tube (G-tube; also known as a feeding tube inserted directly through the abdomen into his belly). My hopes are that within the next week, he will take his bottle again. However, since his tooth popped, he literally screams all night long. We have gotten NO SLEEP. I feel so bad for him, and I just don't know what else to do. I mean, what is a pain and fever reducer going to do when this kid is used to the heavy, duty stuff? I try a frozen washcloth and popsicles for his mouth. He hates the popsicles. I asked the doctors if he could have a gum pain reliever, but it can shed his gums, so that's a no. Teeth suck! But the word on the street is that we get to leave the hospital by the end of next week and move back to the apartment! I'm not going to press my luck, though. Just trying to take things one hour at a time.

Go figure, by the middle of this week Nix lost an entire broviac line. Both lumens stopped working, and now we are down to one broviac with two central lines. He has so many things working against him with these lines. He is so little, he has thin veins, and his meds are sticky. Not much on our side with this one. He will more than likely have surgery this week to get the broken one completely removed. Since he is taking more oral medications, this is usually the plan, but not until they become outpatients. In this case, they do not want to risk an infection adding new central lines. On top of all that, he also now tested positive to a virus that is similar to the common cold. He will be in isolation for the rest of the time he is an in-patient. Awesome.

### Week 12: August 31, 2014

This week, Nixon continues to be very irritable, and we cannot figure out why. He cries just about every 15-20 minutes throughout the day and night. We don't know if it is just "baby" things or if it has to do with the transplant. Back to testing. A CT of his head, x-rays of his chest, abdominal area, hips and arms all came back normal. Back to square one.

We are barely getting any sleep because we don't how to console him. Last night, I tried letting him cry it out. There is no way I am doing that again. It's torture, and after what he has been through, he doesn't deserve it. I want to think that it's normal baby stuff that is bothering him, but I also have to take into consideration that most normal babies don't have stem cell transplants.

Dr. Escolar came in for a checkup, and his progress looks fine. She believes all he needs is therapy to help him get back to where he needs to be. The bone marrow transplant team met. They shared with us that infants and babies get very irritable around this time after transplant, and they can't explain why. It usually lasts a few weeks, so hopefully things will get better soon. As long as everything is okay with him, that is all that we can ask for.

On Friday, Nix had surgery to get his left central line removed. He did amazing, but he has a huge hematoma (a solid swelling of clotted blood within the tissues) where the surgery was. This is common, and we were told not to worry. But it's a big dark purple bruise the size of Texas on his chest. Of course, I'm going to worry! We have one central line down, one to go. We are halfway to home!!

Ozzie and I are very tired. We have been lacking sleep for the past ten days. We get about an average of two hours per night. We definitely have our work cut out for us on a daily routine. Nix takes about twenty different medicines that must be administered either through IV or by mouth. On top of that, we have to continue working with him on physical therapy (stretches, tummy time, sitting up) as well as having him grab things and play with his toys so he doesn't lose that ability. Feeding him is a challenge, but we try about four times a day whether it is by spoon, chewing puffs, or a bottle. He has been eating oatmeal cereal by a spoon and chewing puffs, which is a blessing. He is so close to using his bottle again. As soon as he relearns how to suck on his bottle, he will be there. We may go right to the sippy cup if he doesn't grasp this in a few days.

Before coming to Pennsylvania, we met with pretty much every Gaucher expert in the country. Every single one of those doctors said to us, and we quote, "Your son has a few years at the most. Enjoy him. You are a young family, and you can have more children." However, earlier this week the doctor who oversees the entire transplant team stopped in for a visit and said, "I will be at his high school graduation." You know that feeling where it seems like there is a bowling ball at the pit of your stomach and a jawbreaker is stuck in your throat at the same time because you are trying to hold back the tears from one of the most amazing things that you could possibly hear? Well, that happened. He has given us hope that we can actually hold on to. And we are so happy that we listened to our guts and found this hospital that was able to give him that chance. And even though he has these small hurdles that he needs to overcome, the big picture is that he has a future now.

~

"If your determination is fixed, I do not counsel you to despair. Few things are impossible to diligence and skill. Great works are performed not by strength, but perseverance."

– Samuel Johnson

# Seven

**Week 13: September 7, 2014**

SEPTEMBER ARRIVES WITH A GREAT START. It's Tuesday, and the doctors have given Nixon a pass! This means he can leave the hospital for a few hours, but we have to abide by their rules and make sure we bring him back when they tell us. We walk to the apartment to lay down, and we all take a nap on the big bed together. It is so nice to snuggle with both of my boys! Off to the local superstore chain to pick up a few things. However, Nixon stayed in the car with Ozzie because he cannot yet be in public. He loves riding in the car and is so happy! For a few hours, it feels good to participate in 'real life' outside of the hospital.

We spent Wednesday and Thursday just monitoring Nixon's counts and watching him. Then by Friday morning, Dr. Mark came in and gave us the news that we had waited 82 days to receive. Nixon will be released from the hospital! We can settle into the apartment as a family! It isn't home, but it's a step closer. When a patient is finally able to leave 9B, all of the doctors and nurses give them a parade. This way, we all know how truly special it is to have reached the point where they are finally able to leave. It is so amazing to watch the team that helped him as they cheer him on as Ozzie and Nix walk out the door. I'm in the hallway with the video camera – Geek Mom! Ozzie dressed him in plaid suspenders and a checkered green and blue bow tie. When they walk out, I can't help but notice that Nixon looks so stinkin' cute! Ozzie holds him in his arms facing forward as if he is "King of the World." Colorful balloons in all sizes and shapes line the hallways. As they walk past, confetti cascades around them, and the blare of the noise makers signals it's a celebration of momentous occasion. Through his pacifier, Nixon just smiles at everyone as if he knows that this event is so special. And he is right. I'm thinking the same thing, as the tears just roll down my face. It is so unbelievably remarkable.

Being outpatient status has its pros and cons. The good part is that we can act as a family in our own space. The bad part is the amount of medicine that needs to be administered throughout the day. He gets six oral medicines in the morning, his inhaler, a shot in the leg, two medicines that are administered through his central line, and six other oral medications at night. On top of that, the feedings and physical therapy he needs us to do with him. We also have to find time to feed ourselves, shower and do laundry! By Sunday, we are finally feeling a little bit of a routine and finally feel ok about everything we need to do.

As we settled into this next phase of our journey, as Nixon's new medical team, I had a few moments to think about what my life used to be like and how I took things for granted. I used to be one of those people who would complain about going to work or who would hold a grudge at a comment that was made or get angry about something really petty. Now, I feel like anyone who gets to go to work and have a normal life should consider themselves lucky and count their blessings. I have been feeling so alone lately. It's probably hard to understand what I would give to be around people every day who love and respect me. I miss that connection, the mundane day to day operations, the life that seemed so hard, yet was much simpler than what we have going on now. It's true when they say we really don't know what we have until it's gone. Don't get me wrong, I'm grateful to be here with Ozzie and Nixon. I just really miss the other people in my life that I am used to seeing on a regular basis. The days here are hard (understatement), grueling is more like it. And I'm grateful we have what we have. It's so much work for Ozzie and me. Even though I know our lives will not be the same when we eventually do get home, it will still be so nice to be back in Chicago!

**Week 14: September 14, 2014**

September 15th. Our 2nd wedding anniversary. Ozzie and I are at a romantic first clinic visit for Nixon as an outpatient. Clinic is just like a doctor's appointment where they run blood tests, check vitals, etc. to make sure that it is still safe for him to be out of the hospital. There are two waiting areas. The first is the check-in area for the sicker kids who are immunosuppressed, like Nixon. The second one is around the corner and is larger. It has toys, televisions and more seating. Since Nixon was recently released from the hospital, we are to stay in the check-in area because they have to bring Nixon to his room right away.

The clinic looks like a large doctor's office with about twenty rooms down two hallways. However, our visit didn't go as well as we planned. When they assessed Nixon's vitals, they noticed he had a fever. They even checked it a few times just to be sure it was accurate. A fever means an infection, which means having to be admitted to the hospital. Infections with central lines are extremely dangerous and something that the hospital does not take lightly. So back to 9B we went. It's a good thing we did because he ended up having the start of walking pneumonia. Antibiotics were administered immediately and they tested the line for infection. I seriously cannot believe that we were only outpatient for two days! I guess that's why they only allow you to go as far as the apartment connected to the hospital.

This virus ended up causing his counts to be extremely low. When he received his transplant, they saved 5% of the donor cord blood in case he needed a boost. On Wednesday, they decided it was time to use it and take a chest x-ray to see if his lungs cleared up from the pneumonia. His white cells were drastically decreasing on Tuesday, Wednesday and Thursday, so they stopped some of the bone marrow suppression medicine to help increase his counts. It worked a little bit because Friday to Saturday they were elevated slightly. But by mid-day Saturday, he spiked a 102-degree fever which dropped them to zero.

He wasn't himself and was acting so bizarre that there was a point that I thought that he went blind. He wasn't looking at me or focusing on anything I was saying. They cultured his lines again to check for infections and put him on more antibiotics. This was really scary because we didn't know if it was the fever/virus that caused it or if it was a graft issue. A graft issue means that his own cells would be coming back and kicking out the donor cells. They scheduled a bone marrow biopsy for Monday. By Sunday his fever had broken and miraculously, his counts bumped up to 800 on Sunday night! 1500 is a safe range for white blood cells. The doctors believe that the fever caused his counts to drop, so the fact that they went up meant that his bone marrow was responding. They canceled the biopsy. The relief I feel is indescribable. Now, it is back to the waiting game for his cells to slowly start coming back.

I don't get it. He was doing so well! I saw that little glimpse of a light at the end of the tunnel. Then BOOM! A freight train hit us. We go from outpatient living and then to the thought of him almost losing his graft. My stomach hurt so bad from the ups and downs of being on this roller coaster that I literally could have chugged a bottle of liquid antacid.

Week 15: September 21, 2014

Earlier this week Nixon's counts kept fluctuating, but as the days come and go, they are continuing to increase. Some more good news... he did not need a bone marrow biopsy, and it did not end up being graft issue! Thankfully, today, on Thursday night, we are released from the hospital again. Our hectic days are about to resume. I love being outpatient and having our freedom, but GOOD LORD, is it work. Here is a look at our days:

- Wake up at 8am.
- Try feeding Nix.
- Administer six oral medicines, one inhaler breathing treatment, and one shot in his leg.
- Then we attend either clinic or therapy.
- Try feeding him again, after we take down TPN (his iv nutrition).
- Practice more therapy.
- Give him three oral medicines.
- Try feeding him and then, put up TPN.
- Change caps on his lumens.
- Practice more therapy.
- Try feeding him again.
- Bath time.
- Administer five oral medicines, one shot in leg.
- Bed time.

SPOILER ALERT! KRISTIN'S RANT TIME!

And let me tell you, feeding him is NOT easy, especially trying to get him to take the bottle. GOD BLESS wine to get me through. Not to mention he cries 75% of the day and won't let you put him down. And he's connected to a pole. We are just so exhausted. I know once we get used to it, it will get easier but the crying is what is killing us the most. I feel bad because he has bone pain and is not on pain meds anymore. It has to be that; otherwise I have no idea why he's crying so much.

RANT OVER.

Friday is clinic day, and his counts are at 900; still not in the 1500 range, but not zero either. Ozzie and I are so unbelievably careful about staying clean at the multi-family housing accommodations. With so many sick kids, we are extremely cautious about what we touch. We wash our hands about 100 times a day and follow it with hand sanitizer. We also make sure to stay away from anyone who seems like they are sick. We are NOT going to get Nixon sick and have him go through that again. And it paid off! Monday morning his cell count shot up to 2100!!!! We are headed in the right direction, and Dr. Mark is very pleased!!!

**Week 16: September 28, 2014**

The hot days of summer have ended, and fall is upon us. It is our first full week being outpatient and living in our cozy apartment. The apartment is small, but livable. It has one bedroom, one bath, a living room and a kitchen with a fridge and microwave. The last time my parents visited, they brought us our crockpot, so it was nice to make a couple of home-cooked meals. Nix can't be in public or around crowds of people. We are thankful that we have our car. Every once in a while, to get out of the house and do something different, we go for a drive or have picnics in our car. We have taken him for a walk in the park, but we make sure his stroller is completely covered. He refuses to wear a mask. During one of our escapes, we found a restaurant with an outdoor deck by the marina. It overlooks the Allegheny River. When it seems less crowded, we sit outside. It's wonderful and relaxing to just be outside on a beautiful, sunny fall day, even if it is for just an hour. The food was fabulous, and it was my new favorite place in Pennsylvania.

This is a big and busy week. Dr. Mark wants him to attend clinic three times. His white blood cell counts are finally at a stable level. They are not as high as we want them to be, but they are getting there. His spleen is still eating his platelets, so he needs a couple of transfusions. He also starts speech and physical therapy this week. The wing for all outpatient appointments is on the other side of the cafeteria. His speech therapist said that after the transplant, he is doing exceptionally well, considering he did not have a G-tube and was eating by spoon. He does have an aversion to liquids since he won't drink and hates the bath. She wants us to slowly introduce it back to him. We will start spoon feeding him formula, so he can get used to drinking thin liquids. For bath time, we can place his hand in a bowl of water, which will help him get used to the feeling. With physical therapy, his posture is much better, and when we do tummy time on his boppy, he almost crawls over it. Everything takes time and patience, but we are working very hard with him. He is making progress, which is all we can ask!

This week, I am really starting to miss home. I'm lucky enough that we live in a world with facetime and email. I am really missing my friends and family. Facetime is just not the same as being with them. I just can't wait to hug someone and be in the same room with people who I actually love (other than my boys). Nix is doing really well, but hospital life is hard; very hard. Granted, it's not getting any easier, but we are getting more used to it.

We have been here 113 days now and are 84 days post-transplant. I have to say, I hate Gaucher's disease and what it did to my baby. I have been trying so hard to feed him, and I feel like I am not getting anywhere. I literally feel like it's what I do all day long, every day. His speech therapist wants me to try to spoon feed him formula three times a day. The BMT (bone marrow transplant) doctors want me to get about five tablespoons of some sort of food in him like cereal, avocado, beans, hummus; anything high in fat because he is not gaining above 12 pounds. I try to feed him eight times a day, and it takes him an hour each time. Not to mention trying to get him to do physical therapy in between all of this. I feel like he has no time to relax or time to even just be a baby. Frustration doesn't even begin to describe it. My baby is 11-months-old and hasn't met any milestones, yet. I'm literally exhausted from trying. That was when Dr. Mark told me that I need to stop trying so much. He said there must be parts of the day where I enjoy my child, and he's right. I need to just take a step back and breathe for a minute.

Friends, family, and even people who we don't know have said multiple times that what we are doing is inspirational. We can honestly say that we are doing is what any parent would do for their child, and that is, fight for them. We were just lucky enough to find the right people to help us at the right time. We are so thankful for that. And when I get so frustrated, that is what I need to keep remembering.

~

"Do not dwell in the past, do not dream of the future, concentrate the mind on the present moment."

– Buddha

# Eight

**Week 17: October 5, 2014**

LATELY, IT IS STILL A STRUGGLE with feeding Nixon. He has been on TPN for so long, which is not good for his organs, especially the liver. It increases the risk of having liver damage. Infants and younger children are more at risk because they are still developing. Eventually, I need to get him to eat or they will put a G-tube in him. The G-tube is a feeding tube that they will surgically put into his abdomen, so that he can get his formula and medications directly to his stomach. It can be temporary or permanent, depending on if he ever decides to drink. I don't really want that to happen. I know Nixon has the ability to eat; I just know it. I am getting so tired of trying that I don't know how much longer I can keep trying and failing. If getting a G-tube will help give him the proper nutrition he needs to grow and get better, then so be it. I've realized that the most important thing is that his transplant worked, and he is going to be okay. Everything else will fall into place when he is ready.

A positive spin! This week, Nixon's numbers are the highest they have ever been. He is finally at a point where they seem to be at a stable and safe level. He still needs platelets every other day, but they are starting to hold their own. They are just not to a point where he will no longer need transfusions. We can live with that! They even took him off two of his oral medications and his daily shot. Progress! For some reason, with the good, the bad always seems to follow. Nixon developed a mild case of graft versus host disease. They scale it with a 0-4 rating; 0 being the mildest. Fortunately, he is at a 1. They are able to treat it, and we hope it will go away soon.

I hate that we don't know if and how his brain stem was affected. We have an appointment with Dr. Escolar in two weeks. He has been having tantrums a lot lately, and I don't know if it's a neurological thing or a baby thing. He does a high-pitched scream for a good minute, and we can't figure out what he wants. The more I think about it, I don't know if Dr. Escolar will know either. This is going to be a learning process for everyone, as they have never transplanted a child with Gaucher's before. Even if Nixon could tell us that his tummy hurt, it could mean a number of things. He has so much going on right now, that these high-pitched screams are going to remain a mystery.

It is hard to believe that we have been here for 17 weeks. It is almost as if, prior to this, we lived in a bubble at home. You know situations like this exist, but until you are surrounded by it, you don't believe how common it is, especially when you hear the word 'rare.' What we see every day breaks our hearts. Sick children are the last thing that you want to see every time you turn your head. It's amazing to think about the capabilities that modern day medicine can do now. Some people know what we are going through, and others may never know. One thing that I have learned through this experience is to hug your loved ones tight tonight, and always cherish them. Focus on the positives every day, and try not to think of the negatives. That is what we are doing, and it's the only way we are getting through this journey. One of the most positive outcomes we have is Nixon's attitude. His smile is what keeps us going. He continues to fight to get better and it shows every day!

## Week 18: October 12, 2014

It has been an uneventful weekend filled with eating. We decided to take Nixon for a drive, bought some lotto tickets and ate a late lunch in the car. I found a place that had a sandwich similar to my favorite turkey sandwich place back home, and I am in heaven. While we were at clinic last week, we had been talking about bonfires and s'mores. One of the nurses brought me all the ingredients to make s'mores. Since I didn't have a bonfire at my disposal while living in a hospital, I made use of the microwave. I ate four in a matter of a half hour, and then, my stomach hurt. Bad. But it was so worth it! We seriously have nothing else to do but worry and eat here. I have now started to do sit ups every night before bed.

Today is Monday, and it is a landmark day! It is 100 days post Nixon's transplant. HUGE DAY!!! After day 100, he is at less risk because most infections happen in the first 100 days after transplant. This week, they will do a lot of blood tests that will start coming back over the next two weeks. We are checking to see if he is producing the enzyme on his own, confirming he is still 100% donor, and how his bone marrow is doing, etc. They will now start weaning him off of his medicines and see if he is able to hold his own. I'm nervous and excited at the same time. This will hopefully give us a better idea on going home! Dr. Mark said his goal is to get us home by Christmas. Christmas will be doable. It's not the five months that I thought, but I think I can handle it.

The day was brutal at the clinic. Nixon's blood tests were tough. They poked and prodded him all day long. He also lost his voice and just didn't seem like himself. I felt like something was off with him. Well, lo and behold we came to find out that he developed croup. They did a chest x-ray. Dr. Mark viewed it, and said that we caught it early. The poor kid keeps trying to talk and cry, but he can't. I feel so bad! I wish we could have a humidifier in the apartment. It's not possible because bacteria can grow and be harmful to his transplant. Instead, I will make my own steam bathroom and sit in it with him. Dr. Mark started him on steroids and said we need to just keep an eye on him. He also prepared me, yet again, for the possibility of him getting a G-tube. The fact that he doesn't have one yet is amazing because 90% of kids who have had transplants usually have one by now. He still has his liquid aversion but is getting better with his solid food. I have been working very hard with him, but it takes time. I'm starting to realize he has to do it when he is ready. He gave him a few more weeks before making the decision. However, the G-tube would get us home faster because then we know he is getting the nutrition he needs. And we definitely want to go home as soon as possible. We love good ol' PA, but we love Chicago more!!!!

**Week 19: October 19, 2014**

The fall colors outside are in full show, and the football fans are roaming the streets. Football is sort of a big deal here. However, this week is not the week we were expecting. Nix was transferred to the hospital as in-patient. Since he was born, he has suffered from low platelet count. Platelets are needed to clot bleeding. During the week, he had an ophthalmologist appointment where they found hemorrhaging on his optic nerve and retina, due to his low platelets. There was no damage, thank God, but they admitted him. This way, the tests could be done quicker as an inpatient. He needs an MRI to be sure the hemorrhaging in his eyes is not leading to hemorrhaging in his brain.

On Friday, the MRI of the brain and the bone marrow biopsy were completed. So far, everything that they were able to see looked good. He had lots of immature white cells. On the small part of the slide that they examined, they saw NO Gaucher cells. This means no old nor new cells, which is AMAZING. The remainder of the tests will be back next week.

The MRI showed no bleeding in the brain, but it confirmed some pressure behind his optic nerve near his brain. This is common in Gaucher patients and the neurosurgeon found only a light amount of pressure. Most likely, it is due to low platelet count. Thankfully, a spinal tap is not needed. Follow up appointments with the ophthalmologist will confirm no more hemorrhaging in the future. If he continues to hemorrhage, and it is in the wrong place, then there is a possibility he can lose his vision. All of this talk of hemorrhaging makes me nauseous. This is my kid. You don't think about eyes and brains hemorrhaging when you have an 11-month-old. I should be worrying about him falling into a wall while learning how to walk instead of worrying about bleeding in his brain and eyes. I still can't believe this is his life.

Now, the problem we are running into is that his platelets need to be around 75 to be safe, and he is receiving two transfusions per day, to keep it at that level. A count of 75 reduces his risk of hemorrhaging. However, he cannot be transfused twice a day. If he is, we will be here for another year to get it to stay in the safe range.

Our next consideration is a splenectomy where they remove all or part of Nixon's spleen. Babies need their spleen to help fight infections, especially a transplant patient. They can do an embolism where they insert three beads through a catheter into his blood vessel, clot the nerve and have part of the spleen die so that he only has about 25% of the spleen. But, then there is a risk of having that dead part of his spleen in him for the rest of his life. That can be risky. They could remove the entire spleen or take part of the spleen, which would be a cleaner cut than an embolism. However, an actual surgery also runs risks. They are currently weighing out the pros and cons of the three options regarding his spleen. These procedures will help keep his counts up, which will get us home much quicker, maybe even sooner than Christmas. Once they decide which route, it will be within a few days. While undergoing this surgery, they will also put a G-tube in him for feeding. We are in between a rock and a hard place right now, and we need all of the prayers that we can get. His first birthday is Saturday, and this poor kid hasn't caught a break yet.

**Week 20: October 26, 2014**

Earlier this week, the BMT doctors, surgeons, radiologists, and Dr. Escolar held a conference call. His bone marrow biopsy results came back. 90% of his bone marrow is cells, which is amazing because the number is usually never that high. The other 10% is empty space, which is normal, as the bone marrow is still growing. He is still 100% donor, and they found zero Gaucher cells in his bone marrow, which is also fantastic! Now this doesn't mean that all the Gaucher cells are eliminated. There still can be some in his brain or in his spleen. The only way to find out if they are in his brain is to do a biopsy of his brain, and they don't want to do that. Quite frankly, neither do I. We can only hope.

The spleen situation is still undecided. If they do an embolism, it requires a catheter to insert the beads to cut off the blood supply to let some of the spleen die. The risks include infection and neurological disease progression. Dr. Escolar is really worried about this option. If they do nothing, he would need to continue the platelet infusions with a possibility of hemorrhaging in his eyes. This could cause him to lose his vision. The safest option is to try to surgically remove 80% of the spleen with the possibility of removing the entire spleen, if necessary. We agreed with their recommendation. The surgeon who was on the conference call during the discussion said it would be a simple surgery, so he was selected to perform it. While he is in there, he will repair his umbilical hernia and insert the G-tube. They finally talked me into that one. Dr. Mark said that the G-tube will get us home faster, and I'm holding him to that! The surgery will be Monday or Tuesday of next week. Afterwards, he will be in PICU for a few days. Nixon is turning one, and his present is a surgery to remove his spleen and insert a G-tube in his belly. Nice.

We made it to Nixon's first Halloween! He can't trick or treat, and he can't eat candy. This sucks, but I'm going to make the best of a shitty situation. I got him a puppy costume. His tag line will be "I've had a "ruff" year, but I'm still hanging on!" Some of the doctors and nurses dressed up. The BMT patients trick or treated around the halls to collect their candy. We put Nixon in his stroller with his IV poles and all. We wheeled him around to collect his toys and candy. It was cute, and Nixon looked adorable. His Dad was happy to eat all of the candy for him.

As a parent, when your child has their first birthday, it is a HUGE deal. I never thought that we would be celebrating my only child's first birthday in a hospital away from all of our family and friends. This is not how I saw this. It was not a part of my dreams. I want him to have a party, I want him to get all covered in his smash cake. I want him to be surrounded by all of his family and friends. This is not fair. But all in all, it turned out to be a great day, considering he was in this hospital. I had one of the nurses who takes photographs as her hobby, come and take his first birthday pictures. He was pouty during his pictures, but hey, the kid has a right to be! My old coworkers sent him HUGE Disney balloons that were the size of human beings. He received so many cards and presents from all of his family and friends back home. The nurses surprised him with a huge sign on his door as well as a "transplant friendly" smash cake just for him! It was a Chicago football team cake with blue icing. Nixon looked like a blue elf after digging into that one.

~

"Love many things, for therein lies the true strength, and whosoever loves much performs much, and can accomplish much, and what is done in love is done well."

– Vincent Van Gogh

# Nine

**Week 21: November 2, 2014**

THIS IS GOING TO BE THE BIGGEST SURGERY of Nixon's lifetime. All morning, we anxiously wait in his room while the nurse walks through the paperwork with us and preps him for surgery. SURGERY! A big one. I can barely drink my coffee. I definitely cannot eat anything. I just keep pacing back and forth in his room, hoping something will stall it. I'm not ready to let him do this, but it's the best decision for him, his well-being, and his life.

His nurse that morning is as calm as a cucumber. As she preps Nixon, she makes small talk as if this is nothing. She obviously is so used to seeing these kids go through this. She keeps reassuring me that he is in good hands and that he will be okay. She gives me lots of hugs! She wheels his bed out and down the BMT hallway to the surgical floor. Ozzie, my parents and I follow him. As I clutch Ozzie's arm for dear life, tears just roll down my face. I can hardly breathe. Why can't this be me!?

We approach the door to where we part ways. I just keep crying, kissing his head, telling him that I love him. "You are strong, Nixon, and you can get through this. I will be right here when you wake up." He just keeps smiling at me. My sweet baby boy. I burn that image into my memory bank. It's the image I will always remember and never forget. I give him his pacifier, kiss him about five more times on his head. They wheel him away. I watch him until I can no longer see him. Ozzie, my mom, my dad and I are all somber, as they shepherd us to the waiting area in dead silence, except for a few sniffles.

Every time we see the light at the end of the tunnel, it turns dark again. Ozzie and I are a nervous wreck, to put it mildly. Nixon went in for surgery at 12:15pm. It took an hour to administer anesthesia and hook up his IV's for the blood transfusions. His first cut was at 1:15pm.

They promise to provide updates throughout the procedure, and the next one is due in an hour. My right leg won't stop shaking. I can't eat, and my heart feels like it is going to beat out of my chest. Each minute of this hour feels like eternity, until I see the nurse walk through the door; 80% of his spleen is out, and they already fixed his hernia. Good news. They are waiting to see if blood returns to the remaining 20% spleen. The nurse assures us that it was a beautiful cut.

While they wait, they will insert his G-tube. "Nixon is doing great and is stable," she says excitedly. I keep thinking that I wish, in a way, I could be in the viewing room like they have on TV hospital dramas. I would just like to watch everything they are doing and know that my baby is safe. The waiting is agony. However, the more that I think about watching it, I feel the vomit creep into my throat. I am fine here in the waiting room.

Another hour and a half passes by, and the surgeon walks through the door. FINALLY!! If the surgeon is here, then that means Nixon is on his way to recovery. He asks us to follow him into a small little room. He closes the door. Um. What is happening? I look around. I am terrified. He starts out by saying the surgery went exactly how he had planned, and Nixon has 20% of his spleen, the G-tube is in place, and he fixed his umbilical hernia. Music to my ears!

He then said when they extubated him (removed the breathing tube that was breathing for him while under anesthesia), he stopped breathing all together. Heart drop. They had to intubate him again and put him on a ventilator. He is now in the PICU. He believes that it was due to the anesthesia and the pain medicine. As soon as I heard the words "stopped breathing," nothing else registered. That vomit creeps right back into my throat again. My heart is beating so fast in my chest, it feels like it will explode into a million pieces. The tears just flood my eyes. I can't see. I can't think. I want to stop breathing.

On the way to the PICU, I was shivering the entire trek. A part of me can't get there fast enough, but another part of me doesn't even want to see him like that. I walk into his room and just start bawling. He is laying lifeless on the bed hooked up to so many machines, one of which is making his chest rise up and down. He can't even breathe on his own.

I just keep thinking "What the heck did we do!? Why is this happening? He doesn't deserve this! Did we make the wrong decision??" As I sit next to him and rub his head, I whisper, "I'm so sorry, Nixon. I'm so sorry." The tears stream down my face and drop on his gown.

The hardest part of being a parent is watching your child go through something really, really bad, and we can't fix it for him. I have no idea how I am going to fix this. I can't. I know it is out of my hands, and the only one who could fix this is Nixon. Then I snap out of my state of mind. I remember the phrase,

*"In the end, we only regret the chances that we didn't take, and that sometimes against all odds and all logic, we still hope."*

I told Nixon that he needs to prove to me that we made the right decision in all of this. He needs to prove that hope does exist and that if anyone can fight through this, he can. Then, I just laid my head down next to him and cried.

The next day arrives with positive changes as he starts breathing over the ventilator and squeezes Ozzie's finger!! The PICU doctors don't anticipate him getting off the ventilator until, maybe, Friday. Ozzie and I are hanging in there. My parents who came in for his birthday, flew back to Florida today. Yesterday was rough, so it was so good to have them here for their support and love. They are the best parents and grandparents I could ever wish for, and I know we could not make it through this without them.

The doctors are keeping a good eye on his transplant. His numbers (white blood cell, platelets and red blood cell) are all elevated and are within a normal range for the first time. This is such a relief, considering the shape he is in right now. We learned that a part of one side of his lung has collapsed, so it's going to take some time for that to heal and basically, re-inflate. The ventilator will help with that. The plan is to keep him comfortable and get him strong enough, so that they can eventually try to extubate and get him breathing on his own.

He woke up last night, which freaked me out. He opened his eyes, saw me and a tear came down his face. It was agony. They have him in a paralyzed sedation right now to prevent him from pulling out the breathing tube. The harder time will be when he goes through withdrawal as they wean him from his sedation medicine. He will then be weaned off oxygen. He's basically in an induced coma right now. However, the sedation doesn't seem to be phasing him much since he opened his eyes already. I'm just tired of seeing him go through so much. He doesn't deserve this. I knew this was going to be hard, but this is brutal. It's just not fair. This was not a planned part of this transplant.

As the week went on, we realized that his lungs are sicker than we thought. They are filled with fluid, and it causes his body to be puffy. All day yesterday, I told every nurse and doctor that I was worried about it, and they didn't listen. They took an x-ray and you could barely see his ribcage. Luckily, it's not pneumonia. They believe he may have a mucus plug, which is an accumulation of mucus in the airways that can occur before or after surgery. Since he can't cough, it's hard to tell. They turned down the sedation that is making him paralyzed. He is moving a bit and breathing over the ventilator. He barely looks like himself. A new medicine is added to break up the mucus and make it easier to suction.

Since the ventilator is breathing for him, it is helping his lungs heal, so he doesn't have to do the work. His lung will re-inflate once the fluid is gone. Since they weaned him from paralytic, he moves his lips a little, is able to grab my hand, and he even coughed when they suctioned him. He won't open his eyes, though. They have him in arm restraints, so he won't grab the ventilator tube and pull it out. He is still in somewhat of a coma, and they want to keep him that way until they get closer to taking him off the ventilator. Right now, he is stable as far as his ventilator. His rate setting is 24 breaths per minute, and he needs to be at 16 before they try to take the tube out. Yesterday, he was at 32. We made progress. Today, they tried 22, but he didn't tolerate it, so it went back up. We have our two favorite nurses today and tonight, so that gives me so much comfort. Good nurses make a world of difference.

Sunday morning, six days post-op, starts with two practice runs to make sure he can breathe on his own. And he did! He is very awake and alert this morning. He waves his toy, and it seems like it will be a good day. They take him off the ventilator, extubate him, and then, his right lung collapses. Are you kidding me? To help him breathe, they put a mask on his entire face. He cries because he is scared. It breaks our hearts. He eventually became so tired of breathing – it's such hard work for the little guy – that they had to re-sedate him, paralyze him and put him back on the ventilator. My goodness, how much can a little body take? The doctor we have now is very good, and she assures us that he just needs some more time, and soon, he will be ready. As parents, putting our child's life in someone else's hands is the most excruciating sacrifice. It's so hard to let go. But we must trust them. He just needs to get through, hopefully, the last part of this journey. Lord knows that we are tired of being on this roller coaster.

**Week 22: November 9, 2014**

We are now in November, and I realize that the holidays are coming. With the way things have been going lately, I have no predictions about our holidays this year. I have no predictions as to what each day will even be like. You think you get to a good place, and then, all of a sudden something else happens. I know now, I just have to go moment by moment. This is going to be hard.

Another Monday morning in the hospital. Ozzie heads back to the apartment to take his usual shower break. I remain alone with Nixon and our nurse in his PICU room. My little man, who is on very heavy sedation drugs, happens to be wide awake showing off those bright blue eyes. They dart around the room as he takes in his surroundings. He even pulled off his little mitten which he wore so he wouldn't pull out his tube. He waved it in the air like he just doesn't care. No one can believe how he is so alert being on all the medications that he is on. I know this is a good moment, and I know now that I have to hold onto each and every good moment that comes.

In this moment, Nixon is more himself now, than I had seen him in a while. I am standing by his bedside with his nurse. I start to notice Nixon foaming at his mouth. The nurse yelled

"Crap! He tongued out his tube!!" She immediately hits a big red button on the wall, alarms start going off, and I have no idea what is happening. About a dozen doctors and nurses flood into his room. I keep shouting, "He's awake! He knows what is going on. Please don't scare him!" They immediately start giving him more sedation. I call Ozzie. He can barely hear what I am saying, but he could hear the alarms in his room and ran back as fast as he could. I can't watch, as they remove the ventilator out of his throat. He starts calming down. Then, luckily, Ozzie got there. I have to leave. I need a break in the hall because I am the most nervous I have ever felt inside of me. I do not want Nixon to know that I am scared. The ventilator was out, Nixon was in a comfortable state, and they wanted to give him a chance to see if he could breathe on his own. I keep peeking in the room at Ozzie, and he gives me a thumbs up.

A few minutes later Oz came out of the room and told me to turn around. Nixon's oxygen level went from 90, to 80, then to 20 in a matter of seconds, and he turned blue. They started giving him CPR. At that moment, my world stopped. My heart was beating so hard and so fast that I thought it was going to come out of my chest. I closed my eyes and questions kept going through my head. "What were the last words that I said to him? When did I see his last smile? Did I tell him I loved him when I ran out of the room? Was a few minutes ago the last time I was going to see my baby alive?" I drop everything in my hands, hug myself and fall to the ground in tears.

A few minutes pass. Ozzie pulls me up. I am numb. He says, "They got him back. His oxygen level is good. He is back on the ventilator and is alive." I peek into the room, but I still can't see him with the medical team surrounding him. A nurse keeps turning around to reassure us that everything will be okay. They believe that he coded because of the extra sedation they gave him when he self-extubated. Little stinker. They want to give him a couple more days on the ventilator to make sure his lungs are strong enough before they remove it again.

I am completely numb because of what just happened. I sit by his bedside Tuesday, and just watch him like a mama hawk. I cried, and I prayed with everything for him to be well. The doctors don't feel comfortable trying to extubate him yet because they want to just give him a day to rest.

Wednesday morning, they extubate again. They believe his lungs are at the optimum level. He held his own for a while, but he had to be put on a sleep apnea machine at night. This machine pushes his secretions down to help clear his airway to help him breathe better.

Thursday morning, they removed it, and he started to hold his own.

Friday, he spiked a 103-degree fever that kept returning every six to eight hours. The fever caused rapid breathing and had him working harder than normal. At night, they put him back on the machine for a few hours. He became more agitated being on it, so they took him off. He started doing much better. His lungs are finally healed to where they need to be, but he still needs a little help from some high flow oxygen.

The problems we are battling now are his fevers and his kidney functions. The antibiotics that help fight his infection are hard on the kidneys and can cause damage. They stopped the antibiotics. His levels will start to get back to where they need to be without any damage, as they caught it early. A possible cause to all of this could be the Rhino virus (which is like the common cold, but worse). The surgery didn't help matters, as it probably activated it even more. However, they also can't rule out any other infections, and they will test for more tomorrow.

They believe that once the fevers are under control and he is weaned from the oxygen, we can hopefully be released from PICU. On the positive side, while Ozzie and I ordered Chinese food that night, I opened my fortune cookie and it said "The hard times will begin to fade. Joy will take their place." It couldn't have come at a better time.

### Week 23: November 16, 2014

This week continues in the PICU to get everything under control with Nixon. I feel like last week was such a mess. The apnea machine was removed on Monday at 9:30pm, but he started running a fever again. They think he has an infection. They start him on antibiotics and run a bunch of tests.

By Wednesday, his 103-degree fever finally breaks, and they remove the oxygen completely! Then he battles high blood pressure at 120-130; for his age, a high blood pressure is 110. This could indicate some kidney damage from the antibiotics. Fortunately, kidney damage is reversible and his numbers finally normalized.

We have no idea when we will go home. With Nixon things can change within a week, so it all depends. We have four goals before we can go home:

1) Nixon's numbers are within range and stable.
2) He doesn't need transfusions multiple times a week.
3) He can get his broviacs removed.
4) He doesn't keep getting infections.

That's a lot of different scenarios, so we will just have to see and take it one day at a time now.

Thursday = Transfer Day! We are FINALLY released from PICU back to 9B. For the next week or two, they will monitor him to be sure that we are headed in the right direction.

Friday = Food Day! Today, we start feeding him formula through his G-tube. It's taking some time trying to figure out how much is enough for him to handle, but we are getting there. He also started making his own platelets this week! It gave us reassurance that the surgery was the right thing to do. His white cells are starting to stabilize at a normal level.

Saturday = Smile Day! He is finally feeling better. He is more interactive, but fussy. We think it has to do with the feeds going through his G-tube. It could be too much in his belly at once, and they are weaning him from the heavy drugs. The poor guy, he was on so much at one time, so they need to move off slowly. We will see what happens. He actually smiled a few times for us and even gave us high fives! It was such a great feeling! We are coming into the week of Thanksgiving. Throughout this entire transplant process, we have had so much support from our family and friends. It has shown us what the important things are in life, and we have learned so much. The most important thing for which we are thankful, is Nixon.

**Week 24: November 23, 2014**

This is going to be a new experience for us. Spending a holiday while in a hospital. On the bright side, Nixon is having a great week, and Ozzie's parents and brother came in for a few days! His blood pressure is under control, his white cells are at a stable level, and he is finally making and holding his own platelets. We still can't master the G-tube. It's taking some time trying to figure out how much and when the right time is to feed him. We slowly run formula through a pump at a continuous rate. He has become very irritable at night, and we can't figure out why. It's also taking time trying to wean him from the narcotics and find the dose that he can handle to keep him comfortable. It's a lot of trial and error. However, he is enjoying spending the week flirting with his 9B nurses! He's doing so well. Now three new goals:

1) Get the feedings with his G-tube under control.
2) Remove IV fluids.
3) Surgery to remove his central line.

If we meet these goals, there is a possibility of us going home by Christmas. As the holiday season has started, we are starting to get very homesick. We miss our family and friends and want to be home for the holidays. I'm sad because when I go on social media I see everyone getting their Christmas trees, decorating and shopping. Even if we make it home for Christmas, we won't have a Christmas tree at home. My friend, Jamie, reminded me that it will be just that much better when I can have a Christmas tree and decorations. These experiences put life into perspective. When we don't have all that stuff, we can actually focus on the more important things. As much as we want to get back to our regular lives, we are never going to forget that this type of life exists.

~

"The real man smiles in trouble, gathers strength from distress, and grows brave by reflection."

– Thomas Paine

# Jen

## Week 25: November 30, 2014

As December approached, we thought we would start to smell the end of our stay, but it was a heck of a week. On Monday, our discharge papers were in our hands, and we were getting ready to leave on Tuesday. Monday night started with a fever. Since he has a central line, transplant rules dictate that a fever is an automatic two-day stay in the hospital. Every 12 hours, his fevers returned with vomiting and diarrhea. He also needed to be on oxygen because his oxygen levels were not staying where they should. His ANC and white counts were also going down; luckily his platelets remained at healthy levels. Originally, the doctors thought it was aspiration pneumonia. They ran every test they could, and everything came back negative.

By Wednesday, his counts were so bad and he had a fricken 103-degree fever again. He was doing so good before!!!! I just want to cry. It's so lonely here. I just feel so bad for him, and all I want for Christmas is for my son to be healthy. He doesn't deserve this. I don't even care about coming home anymore. Okay, well, I do because I'm extremely homesick, but one thing at a time. We will get through this though; just like we get through everything else.

They have infectious disease doctors come look at him every day. If you thought seeing the surgeon come through the surgery room door was scary... The pulmonary team and the GI team monitor him, in case it is aspiration. No one can figure out what is causing it. They concluded that it must be a virus, which cannot be tested. Again, he is on antibiotics for the next week, and they want him to remain in the hospital. Ugh!!!!

To remove the central line before we leave, he has a feed goal. Through his G-tube his rate must be 25 ml's per hour of a continuous run to get a certain amount of calories per day. He is currently at 18, so we are making progress!

Ozzie has been on FMLA (Family Medical Leave Act benefits) from work and now needs an extension, as we had no idea how long this was going to take. We have so much to figure out when we do get home. We need to find a house, since we gave up our apartment. We will most likely need home nursing, medical equipment, therapies and who knows what else. I don't even know where to begin when that happens. Thinking about it makes my stomach hurt. We had to see Dr. Mark for a realistic release date, so we could get Ozzie's extension and start planning. He told us to tell them March 1st. What!? March 1st!? That is three months from now!!! I want to punch him in the face.

### Week 26: December 7, 2014

It's a beautiful day in 9B. Shouldn't it B? Nixon continues antibiotic treatment to control his fevers. Miraculously, his BMT numbers are consistently amazing. A normal platelet level is 150, and on Tuesday they were 234. His white counts have also been much higher than a normal level. We are so thankful for that.

On Wednesday, Nixon made it through the whole night without needing oxygen! So, I spent Thursday having a Mommy and Nix day while Ozzie went on a field trip. The hospital shuttled a group of parents to breakfast, then to an outdoor mall and, gave everyone a $200 gift card for Christmas presents for their child. Ozzie did a wonderful job. He found Nixon his own toy medical bag. He can take his own temperature and blood pressure. He also found a few other toys and a ton of clothes. Ozzie also brought home toys for some of the kids on the floor. Some of our friends from home sent us money to buy gifts for Nixon's floormates, as well. People are so generous. Later that day, a Pennsylvania hockey team came by to visit the kids. We met them and they held Nixon for pictures. We are huge fans of Chicago's hockey team, so it was really cool to see some of the hockey players, even if they weren't from our own team.

Friday, they did Nixon's bone marrow biopsy and found NOT A TRACE of Gaucher's cells in his bone marrow!! It fricken worked!! I still can't get over that they did it. They possibly cured this horrible disease from him. Dr. Escolar said she does see some neurological effects, but nothing that cannot be managed. He is doing great. He smiles, laughs, grabs, and puts things in his mouth. He can almost sit up without help. He is very deconditioned from being in a hospital bed for six months, but with therapy, they think we will eventually get to walking. He even put his mouth around his sippy cup and will eat cookies all on his own. I also swear he said "Hi" the other day.

The plan for the rest of the week is to finish his antibiotics and release us from the hospital on Monday. Lo and behold, Sunday night Nixon spiked another fever. We are pretty sure our new permanent residence is 9B in Pennsylvania's finest hospital. They cultured his central line and discovered that he has a blood infection. He is back on antibiotics and the goal is to have surgery to get his central line removed sometime next week. If it's not one thing, it's another, and we are about to go crazy!

## Week 27: December 14, 2014

The start of our 27th week was pretty scary. Nixon's blood infection caused him to get septic shock episodes. This causes drastic changes in the body. Infections are bad for BMT patients. The one he has is common, and he seems to be responding to antibiotics. They just need to get that central line out because we believe that is what is causing it. He got another fever, threw up, had a rapid heart rate, started shaking uncontrollably, and then would get incredibly stiff to the point of where we couldn't even move him. I just sit there and hold him until he stops shaking and eventually falls asleep. Why does this keep happening to him!? Once his medicine starts working, he eventually calms down and falls asleep. He had one of these episodes Sunday night, Monday, and Tuesday morning. However, his ANC is over 15,000 (which is normal range) and his platelets are 234! So, I'm pretty excited about that.

By Tuesday, both lumens were infected in his broviac. This is so dangerous because blood infections could ruin everything. They have him as an 'add-on' to have surgery to get the line out immediately. We are really nervous because he has not done well with breathing during surgery. I'm a wreck.

At 1:42pm, they take him for surgery. I hate that he was going into it with a fever, but they started him on double antibiotics. That line needs to get out before it puts anymore bacteria in his body. I pray he can do this. When the doctor came out around 5:15pm, he told us it was done. Luckily, they were able to do the surgery with an intubation method that didn't go past his vocal cords. They removed the central line and added a PICC line. A PICC line looks like an IV in the arm. However, it has a catheter to transmit medications directly to his heart through an IV. But he did it! He returned to his room and was resting comfortably. THANK GOD!

Ever since his central line has been removed, he has not had any fevers and has been responding like a champ. He even said his first word this week! "Hɪ!" It was confirmed that the transplant fixed his blood cells, and he is now producing the enzyme that will stop any new Gaucher cells from producing. At least that is the hope. They don't know for sure, but it has worked on Krabbe disease patients which is similar to Gaucher's disease in some respects. All tests are pointing in the right direction! He will always have Gaucher's disease, but we hope that the transplant eliminates the effects of the disease. Similar to how Ozzie and I both carry the Gaucher's gene. It's in our DNA, but it does not affect us. We hope that this will be the case for Nixon. The disease could still have affected him in some parts of his body, especially his brain. It's still in his skin and in his genes, but not in his blood. In two months, he has progressed six months in gross motor skills. According to the test from his therapists, he is at the development level of a 11-13 month-old, except in language.

The holiday season is a perfect time to reflect on our blessings and seek out ways to make life better for those around us. I keep telling myself how lucky we are to have so many people in our lives that have been so supportive.

**Week 28: December 21, 2014**

The week of Christmas is finally upon us. Nix has been so fussy, and we just can't figure him out. He went to bed last night at 5:30am and was bright-eyed and bushy-tailed at 9:06am. I want to fall over. Tonight, I am awake at 3am because Nixon's pump keeps beeping and woke up the little monster. He decides he doesn't want to stop screaming at the top of his lungs. He thinks it's fun. He really has grown fond of his own voice! Somehow, I figured out that by 1pm on Monday, Ozzie and I have slept a total of 5 hours in the past 48. On the upside, in a couple of hours Nixon will be released from the hospital!!!!

We have settled back into the apartment. It has been quite an adjustment because Nix was super fussy at the end of last week and at the beginning of this week. We believe it could be fatigue from being in a hospital room for 6½ months and a change in atmosphere is in order. Or it could be neurological. He has been awake and screaming now for three nights. It's a high-pitched scream that just doesn't stop, and quite frankly, it's annoying. My one girlfriend wrote an email saying she gave her son acetaminophen for the second time, and he's two years old. If my friends knew how many times Nixon has received that, they would crap themselves. Not to mention all the other stuff that he is on. I'm going to give him a detox when this is all over.

On Tuesday, on a whim, we decided to bring Nixon out. We took him to the Flight 93 memorial. It was a mess. It was a two-hour drive, and Nixon threw up in the car on the way there and upon our arrival. The weather was cold and crappy, so we stayed a whole ten minutes and drove two hours back.

We thought we would be clever and try it again on Wednesday. We headed to surrounding towns to view their beautiful Christmas lights. On the internet, Ozzie found a five mile stretch of lights that ended with a winter wonderland. Nixon loves lights so this was perfect, and it wasn't too far. We drove, drove and drove, in the fricken dark, with no lights. Why? Well, after we came home, I jumped on the website. This spectacular light show was from three years ago. So that was yet, another "successful" adventure.

On Christmas morning, we wake up in Pennsylvania, which does not make me happy. A knock on our door, and it's as if Santa arrived. Volunteers walk in with bags of presents donated, not only for Nixon, but for Ozzie and me as well. I'm completely overwhelmed by this kindness. We are actually able to celebrate Christmas with our little mini Christmas tree in our home away from home. As crappy as our situation is, it still feels like

Christmas. We don't have any Christmas dinner plans, so we decide to eat at a local Italian eatery. Nix did fabulous, and we even enjoyed our meal. After dinner, we visited the nurses at 9B, opened presents back at the apartment, gave Nix all his medical stuff and went to bed. He slept nine hours straight that night, and so did we! Merry Christmas!

After a few days of getting into a routine, he is finally calming down. He is even happy at times. During clinic this week, we found out that Nixon's numbers are finally back to a normal range, since they dropped so low from his infection. He finished his antibiotics on Friday, so we are hoping that his fevers do not come back. Fingers crossed that the infection is gone. The rest of the weekend went very well. For next week, we hope he can get his PICC line removed, and we can get the OK to finally go home!

We are truly happy to see this year come to a close, as it has been the hardest year that we have ever had to endure. However, this year has also been a huge eye opener for us. When you think that there is no more hope, look deep inside your soul, because somewhere inside, you will find a miracle. And that is what we will hold onto when we look back on 2014.

~

"Permanence, perseverance and persistence in spite of all obstacles, discouragements, and impossibilities: It is this, that in all things distinguishes the strong soul from the weak."

– Thomas Carlyle

# Eleven

**Week 29: December 28, 2014**

THINKING BACK, I realize that Ozzie and I have been together for 20 hours a day for the past seven months. It tends to be a lot sometimes. In his whole life, Nixon has lived in Pennsylvania longer than he has lived in Chicago. I think that is just crazy! If Nixon gets a fever between tomorrow and Monday, we will have to stay because that means he has an infection. Once the PICC line is out, (hoping on Monday), then fevers won't be as big of a deal because he won't have a line going right to his heart. They will remove it while we are at our clinic appointment. They pull it out like a string of spaghetti. I may barf. So long as Nixon does not get any fevers, we are getting everything packed up this week. When we go to clinic on Friday morning, I'm telling Dr. Mark that we are leaving. My parents are driving up this week, and I'm hoping that they can just take us with them when they leave. They will have room in the car for our stuff, and it will be safer having them follow us home. It just makes sense. It takes seven hours to get home, and without stopping we could be home by Friday night. Depending on how Nix does, we may have to stay somewhere for one night. We will then be home on Saturday. I know it's a long shot considering Dr. Mark told us that we are probably going to stay until March, but I'm still going to prepare and get ready. He needs to just go home. Kids always do better when they are home. So that's MY plan!

No fevers! It's Monday! At clinic, they remove his PICC line; I left the room. That stuff is just gross. I told Dr. Mark that I was getting ready to leave this week. If all his numbers are in good ranges and he looks good, we are hitting the road! He laughed and made no promises. I'm fine with that though, because he did not say "No Way." So, there is still hope!

When we returned to the apartment, I was playing around on the internet. I came across a professional blogger and photographer who wrote the most poignant poem I have ever read. Lexi Griffin Behrndt touched my heart and inspired me to share my thoughts and feelings with Nixon's Medical Team.

Lexi wrote, "An Open Letter to My Son's Medical Team." Although, I didn't write it myself, it was every word that I wanted to say to Nixon's Medical Team. Lexi Griffin Behrndt, mom and blogger at ScribblesAndCrumbs.com, Thank you for permitting us to use your letter in our book. You eloquently put into words, what I cannot. It's an honor to share this here and show our deep gratitude to Nixon's doctors, nurses, techs and everyone involved in his medical care.

*"An Open Letter to My Son's Medical Team"*

*To My Son's Medical Team,*

*He may be just another baby, and we may be just another set of parents. But to us, you are so much more.*

*You are the ones that sat us down and told us that his chances were slim, and anyone else may not have given him a chance. You did it with compassion and bravery.*

*You are the ones that labored over him day and night, watching monitors as his saturations and pressures would drop, pushing his meds, calling doctors, tweaking his vent, bagging him, giving him treatments, and giving him your very best.*

*You are the ones that answered our endless questions with diagrams, print-outs, drawings, and long words that seemed like a foreign language to us. You tolerated and had patience with our run-ins with google and our paranoid questions and concerns.*

*You are the ones that rounded every morning, going through a normal routine, and then breaking it just for a minute to get a laugh or smile from him.*

*You are the ones that taught us how to care for him, with great patience and detail. You gave us little jobs that allowed us to take part in his care and feel more like his parents and less like helpless bystanders.*

*You are the ones who talked to us like we were a human, not just a patient's parents who were trapped in a hospital for seven months. You gave us a chance to have a normal conversation.*

*You are the ones who went the extra mile, googling and researching his various infections in your free time and calling in on your days off to check in on us.*

*You are the ones who took him on, not knowing entirely what you were getting yourself into, and yet you loyally and lovingly and skillfully walked beside him, every step of the way, even if it meant getting your heart involved.*

*You are the ones who learned him and you trusted us enough to take us seriously when we had a bad feeling or when we thought he didn't look well. You allowed us to be parents that knew their baby.*

*You are the ones that made the tough decisions when we couldn't make them ourselves. You are the ones that we trusted in the difficult moments and the ones whose counsel we sought.*

*You are the ones who believed in him even when no one else did and fought to give him a chance countless times.*

*To us, you are the brave ones. The strong ones. You are the ones who choose to work in a place where you witness things that people should not witness on a daily basis. You go where others will not or cannot go, and the best go there with love and compassion.*

*What you do matters in more ways that just the physical act of working to save a life. What you do matters so much more than that. You are saving and literally changing lives.*

*Anyone can be smart. Anyone can be skilled. Anyone can be good, but the best become the best by putting their heart on the line. The best are the best because of the little faces and little stories that are forever etched in their memory as a reminder of why they do what they do and why they return to work, even on the hard days.*

*He had the best. You are the best.*

*He may be just another baby, and we may be just another set of parents. But to us, you will always be so much more.*

- Written by Lexi Griffin Behrndt & shared with permission by Kristin, Ozzie and Nixon Skenderi

It is New Year's Eve, and my parents will arrive this afternoon. We started packing this morning. Like I said, I know it's a long shot, but I don't care. I would rather be prepared. In two days, on Friday, we have to go to clinic, so he can hopefully get his last round of IVIG (which helps for graft versus host disease) and to get some final information from Dr. Mark and his staff.

Usually, on New Year's Eve, I'm getting all dolled up ready for a night of drinking. This one is so completely different. We didn't do much, just went to dinner and came back to the apartment. My mom brought Nixon some glow sticks, so he waved those in the air. None of us made it to midnight.

New Year's Day is boring this year. We don't have much to do, so we just eat, hang out and pack some more. We are all anxiously awaiting Friday's clinic session. His numbers HAVE to be good tomorrow. They just have to!

I feel like a child on Christmas morning. It's Friday! Finally! I can't shower and get ready fast enough to leave for the clinic. As Ozzie, Nixon, my parents and I walk through that bridge from the apartment to the hospital, I pray that this is the last time I have to make the walk past the cafeteria through the double doors and up the elevator to 9B. It is actually kind of eerie doing it, and I have a pit in the bottom of my stomach like you wouldn't believe. We check in with the girls at the front desk who adore Nixon. He flirts with them, of course. We only have to wait a few minutes until they call us into the last room on the left. Dr. Mark walks in, and I just look at him feeling a million different things. He looks at me and says "So, are you ready to go home today?" The tears just start flowing. I can't believe it! Finally! Dr. Mark said that his numbers came back great. He just needs to give him his IVIG treatment, which will last about an hour. And then, we are hitting the road! We must return to PA for a follow-up appointment in a few months.

As his treatment is flowing in, I just sit there and watch. It can't flow fast enough. While that was happening, Ozzie and my parents are packing the car, so after this was done, we could just hop in the car and start driving. We needed to drive through Pennsylvania, Ohio, Indiana and then into Chicago. His treatment finally finished about 11:00am. We gave our hugs to everyone. I couldn't hug them any tighter or they would burst. And Dr. Mark is not a hugger, but today he made an exception. I will be forever grateful to this team. As we walk through the clinic, down through the elevators and through the lobby one last time, I can't help but think of this amazing accomplishment that Nixon has achieved. It makes me so unbelievably proud. I can't stop crying. We hop in the car, buckle everyone in and start to caravan HOME!

Once we saw the sign to Ohio, I took a picture of it and sent it to Dr. Mark. I want him to know we made it out of the state. Nixon is doing very well in the car, surprisingly. We keep him busy with singing, watching TV and reading him books. When we reached the border of Ohio and Indiana, we decide to stop for a bit. We grabbed some food, filled up gas, got out of the car and made the decision to drive through the night until we get home. You don't mess with a good thing, and he was doing good. The drive through Indiana felt like forever. It is boring and feels like the longest stretch of road. I wish I could just snap my fingers, and we would be home.

Then, finally I see the Chicago skyway toll bridge. My city! It's been so long!!! My heart is pounding. It is about 7pm, and I can't stop staring out the window. This is everything that I know, everything I missed. I didn't know if I would ever be seeing it with Nixon again. In about one hour we will be pulling down our street. As we drive down Interstate 90, I look at all of the billboards and familiar buildings that I used to pass driving from the city to the suburbs. So much of it is still the same; yet everything is different.

Last year, when we left Chicago, Nixon didn't have a chance. Today he does. We finally reach our exit. My heart is about to beat out of my chest. Again. In a good way, this time. All of a sudden, as we exit the highway, my focus turns to a popular song on the radio by a famous female recording artist. This song is going to stick with me forever, and will always remind me of this moment. Even though the song is about a relationship, there is one phrase in it that will always remind me of Nixon, what he went through and that our journey could have gone either way. And yes, it's absolutely 100% worth it; it's going to be forever; and it was definitely worth the pain. We pull down our street, and I see something. A crowd of people shadowed from our headlights stand in front of our house. As we get closer, and the headlights of the car shined on them brighter, I see all my friends. They are standing in the middle of the street cheering with signs. Ozzie said, "What the hell!" I just tell him, "Stop the car as soon as you can." He pulled in the driveway, as they all followed. I literally jump out of the car, hug the first person I could get my hands on and start sobbing. They all just huddle around us and start crying. It is amazing to actually hug the people who mean so much to me after everything we have been through. It means everything, and I can't believe that we did what we did. It was the best homecoming!

After chemotherapy, an actual transplant, six surgeries, countless MRI's and CT scans, five weeks in the Pediatric Intensive Care Unit, being on a ventilator, and even needing to be resuscitated, Nixon has shown us that he is the strongest person that we know. It has been seven long months, and Nixon is finally where he belongs; back in "sweet home Chicago!" As this disease is so rare and transplants are never done, the doctors cannot predict the future. But at the start of it all, Nixon lacked an enzyme that our brains need for proper development. At the end of our Pennsylvania journey, his body now produces that enzyme and is sending it to his brain all on its own. He also shows no sign of Gaucher cells in his bone marrow. Just the fact that those two things are possible is extraordinary. He fought through it all, and he made it. Through all of this, this kid taught me to live harder, to love harder, to laugh harder and to fight harder. We fought for our son, we didn't give up, and we saved his life.

~

"It was the best of times, it was the worst of times."

"Whatever I have tried to do in life, I have tried with all my heart to do it well; whatever I have devoted myself to, I have devoted myself completely; in great aims and in small I have always thoroughly been in earnest."

– Charles Dickens

# Twelve

WE ARRIVED HOME TO CHICAGO on January 2, 2015 and began transitioning into "Special Needs Parents." Saying the words, "I have a special needs son" for the first time was really hard, but eventually, it became very normal. Unbeknownst to us, our vocabulary started to sound like we were now medical professionals, which was key to Nixon's survival. We started our new norms in our new world.

We need the first two months to get ourselves in order and adjust being back in our lives again. I am an emotional mess. Early Intervention services is a support and educational system through the state for children who have developmental delays or disabilities. They came to the house to interview Nixon. It is a very in-depth evaluation that feels invasive and judgmental. I'm not trying to knock what they do and what they offer. Their talents and offerings are remarkable. When your child is being evaluated for everything he is not doing right, it is like no other experience. In addition, the amount of therapy and equipment that he needs is beyond overwhelming.

When we left for Pennsylvania, we gave up our apartment, so when we came home, we moved into my parents' house. Five people in a three bedroom house with boxes of our belongings everywhere is a little tight. Just the thought of all the equipment he will need makes it feel even more cramped.

We need a house, but Ozzie needs to get back to work before we could even start working on finding a house. He works for the City of Chicago which means we need to maintain our residency in the city for him to return to work. We can't get a place to live without paychecks, and he can't get a paycheck without going back to work, so we are in a bit of a pickle. He is applying for a three-month waiver to allow us to stay with my parents while we look for a house. We are definitely in a time crunch. An apartment isn't ideal because it has to be clean enough for Nixon. With a transplant, I want a clean environment, and I want a place where we can stay and not move again. I have always been one who has a handle on things; money in the bank, preparing for what could happen, a plan for "just in case," and stability. I am actually really scared because we have no income and no plan. Believe it or not, things were so much easier in good ol' PA than they are now because the only thing we had to worry about was Nixon. Now we have everything else.

I am holding on to good things again. Take each moment as it comes! Nixon is starting to sit up on his own without help! It's on the couch, not on the floor, but it is a huge deal! We hit the jackpot when we found Dr. Frank, our new pediatrician. He is close by where we plan to live. We absolutely love him. He has been very welcoming to a patient like Nixon. He is so interested in his medical history. We felt like we have a Dr. Mark and a Dr. Escolar at home. Weekly blood tests are confirming his numbers are stellar, so far. As they remain where they need to be, we will have to go less frequently. He has been quite fussy since we returned home. It could be anything, really - adjusting to a new environment, teething, growing, gas, his formula or sleep, which is something that the three of us are not getting. We met with Early Intervention again, and we love the team that will be working with him. Now that we are past the evaluation phase, I don't feel as vulnerable, plus we are adjusting to this new life pretty well. It's all for Nixon. The full plan is incredible and gives us much hope that he will continue to improve and get healthier. He will be getting physical therapy twice a week, speech twice a week, developmental therapy once a week, occupational therapy once a week, nutrition once every two weeks and developmental vision therapy once every two weeks. We look forward to starting because the more therapy he gets, the more he can advance. All in all, we hope everything runs as smoothly as possible.

As February hits, sleeping is our number one battle. Nixon is having GI issues. Dr. Frank advises bland foods to let his digestive system get back on track. An upset stomach could be causing him not to sleep. I am at a breaking point, and I don't know what to do. I've been going on a week of not sleeping and trying just about everything. Lavender essential oil, a special teething bracelet, a "magical" sleep sack, pain reliever, stronger pain reliever, frozen pacifiers, walking up and down the hallways bouncing him, letting him cry. Nothing is working, and we still are trying to find a place to live. I started thinking that I was being punished because we didn't travel the route we were told to follow and saved his life. I thought that we were already given more than what we could handle and just when I thought things couldn't get any worse, they did. My silver lining at the end of each day is knowing that Nixon is alive. Had we not done what we did then, he would not be in the place that he is in at this moment. Things could have been a lot worse. I keep thinking about the kids that I was around every day last year. They have a difficult life in the hospital, and they smiled every day. It is the only thing keeping me going.

Nixon's therapists now come to the house. He did very well the first couple of weeks, but then, he ended up in the hospital with the stomach flu and pneumonia. Being back in the hospital is surreal, it was too soon, and it scared me. He did get better and luckily enough, we are going home after only a few days. It set him back about a week, but he is now able to continue with his therapy. We are spending the end of March and April actively looking for a house. Luckily, we found one!

By the end of May, we bought our first house, which included Nixon's very own therapy room. We spent the first few weeks of June moving. Then we had to head to Pennsylvania for Nixon's first follow-up appointment. It's hard to believe the time has come to head back.

As the nice weather of June was upon us, we boarded our flights to PA. Being back is bittersweet. A part of me is relieved that this will be a short stay, but when I walk into that hospital again, I'm hit with a flood of memories. It gave me goosebumps. He went to a therapy evaluation, which showed he improved from a nine-month level to one-year-old level. The fact that he improved developmentally is amazing. An extensive MRI showed how the disease has affected his brain, and we are happy to report that it came out stable. This means that if there are any Gaucher cells left in his brain, then they have not caused any more damage and they do not believe it will in the future. It also is reason to believe that the enzyme he was lacking before, is now getting to his brain. A spinal tap found no pressure around his brain. Neurologically, he could not be doing any better.

A pulmonary lung function test showed some obstruction in his lungs and asthma like symptoms, so he will remain on his inhaler. Regarding his transplant, all of his numbers have been in a normal range, except for his liver, which they believe was caused by the disease. We just need to continue to keep an eye on it. Later in the week, we learned that his chimerism test came back once again as 100% donor, which means the chance for a relapse at this point is very small. However, we aren't out of the woods until two years post-transplant. The doctors told us we can slowly start weaning him off all medicines, so he will only remain on vitamins. He significantly improved on his speech and oral feedings but still gets about 80% of his nutrition through his G-tube. With therapy and all the equipment he is getting in the next month or so, we hope Nixon will continue to improve as best as he can. We rocked this trip!

We make it to July, and I start getting very emotional. I think it is because Nixon's transplant anniversary is in a week. I still can't believe everything that we went through. Just thinking about how our life was a year ago, it's just unbelievable. I start going through pictures, and it seems like it was yesterday. It makes me miss the doctors, nurses, the families and the kids that we met. Nixon never had a first birthday party, and in the "transplant world" they call transplant day a "re-birthday." We decide to give Nixon the biggest, most best birthday party that we can. We will have it at my parents' house. We send out invitations for over 200 people. It will be an all-day affair with a huge bouncy house, water sports, a face painter, and TONS of food and drinks. Being around everyone that supported and loved us through this journey was exactly what we needed. The weather was amazing. It was a great turnout, and all in all, a perfect day.

Nixon's equipment was finally delivered at the end of July. He has a stander, which will help his muscles grow properly and allow him to put weight on his legs and feet. Hopefully, one day he will be able to stand and walk on his own. He also has a kid cart, which puts him in a proper sitting position so that his joints and head position are all where they should be. On top of those two very important pieces of equipment, he has hand splints (to help him from making a fist which he does all the time), an abdominal binder (to help give him abdominal support), AFO's (to control position and motion of the ankle, compensate for weakness and correct deformities), a SPIO vest (which provides deep pressure to help with trunk control), and leg immobilizers (which help to support his knees and legs so they don't buckle when he tries standing). He also has glasses! Gaucher's disease causes strabismus, which misaligns his eyes so they are crossed inward. We are hoping these will help with his vision and maybe even work on making his eyes a little bit more centered.

I am so tired of this August heat in Chicago, so I decide to sign Nixon up for swim classes. It gets us out of the house and helps get him involved in something socially. He feels indifferent about it; he doesn't love it, nor does he hate it. I think he enjoys when he floats on his back or tummy. It made me realize that I had to brush up on my nursery rhyme songs that they sang. I swear they changed the words to half of them since I was a kid.

By mid-August, everything starts going downhill for us. We thought Nixon just caught the flu, until he ended up throwing up 17 times in one day. I was driving to a play date and had to pull over on Interstate 90 while it was under construction because he started choking on his vomit and turning blue. I took him to the ER, and he was admitted because he was extremely dehydrated. They started doing tons of tests to figure out what was going on with him.

While I am there, I am losing my marbles from being back in the hospital. I feel like I am back in jail and have no idea when we are going to be able to leave. After four days of being in the hospital and not being able to figure out what was causing him to throw up, they did an upper GI test. It showed an obstruction of scar tissue in his small intestines from his splenectomy that he had last November. They took him to surgery, which lasted about three hours and repaired it all. When he started having bowel movements, they started slowly feeding him electrolytes and then a thicker liquid and then food. It is such a slow process. It's exhausting because doctors, nurses and specialists are in the room every ten minutes. We are always taking two steps forward and five steps back. I just want to start enjoying life with my baby. We've been here a week and can now go home. Nixon is starting to slowly return to his normal self. That was, at least for a couple of weeks.

We always knew that Nixon had muscle spasms, and that he twitches in his sleep. But it wasn't until we started weaning him off of his medicine from the abdominal surgery that we realized how bad it was. After sending videos to his doctors and going for an EEG, we found out that Nixon was having seizures. We aren't sure if these just started or if he was always having them, but they were masked by his medicine. We now see a neurologist here in Chicago who is keeping in contact with Dr. Escolar. Nixon had a 30-minute EEG, a 24-hour inpatient EEG, as well as a 48-hour at-home video EEG. After going through all the tests, we discover Nixon was having about 30-40 seizures per night. We didn't want to put him back on the medicines because we didn't necessarily know if those were the right medicines for the types of seizures that he was having. He started on a seizure medication that we weren't very happy about because after a couple of weeks of being on it, we noticed he just wasn't himself. I've accepted that my life is going to be in and out of hospitals, and I am okay with that. As long as Nixon gets to experience life, that is all that matters. We need to get these seizures under control, so he can start doing things again. Then the unthinkable happened. We attempted to take Nixon out to dinner with my parents. He started acting not himself, and luckily we were not far from home. We left the restaurant and went home, since all of Nixon's equipment was there and we felt safer. On the way home, he turned blue. I immediately put my mouth on top of his and gave him some breaths. I grabbed him out of his car seat and started pounding on his back to which his color finally came back and he started breathing really slowly.

I call 911, and had an ambulance meet us in front of our house since we were a minute away. We made it before the ambulance arrived, so Ozzie was holding him in his arms in the front lawn bouncing him up and down so he would keep breathing. All of a sudden, he turned limp and blue. Ozzie laid him on the ground and started CPR. I panicked, but I could hear the sirens coming closer. I rang the neighbors' doorbells and yelled help while my body was shaking uncontrollably. Not sure what they could do, but it was out of instinct. I guess it made us feel that we weren't in it alone. Ozzie's CPR helped him breathe again just before the ambulance arrived. I didn't think I would ever be in that place of fear again. This was an extreme eye opener for us, and we are not going to be ok until we get these seizures under control.

We were in the hospital for about a week when they decide to wean him from the current meds and start him on a new one. They also believe that the seizures are causing him not to sleep, and not sleeping also causes seizures, so it's a catch 22. I feel so bad for him. He has no control of what his body is doing and tries so hard to fight it. Yet he still smiles. He will even smile through a seizure because that's just the kind of kid he is. It's just so difficult adjusting and figuring out what medicines are right for him. We have a trip planned for October to California to take Nixon to Disneyland and San Diego. We are now contemplating calling it off, but Nixon needs to experience life and we really need this trip. At this point a change of scenery is exactly what we all need. Who knows? It may help.

Our vacation to California has been wonderful! Nixon is so happy all the time. First, we went to Disneyland, and he slept for six hours straight that night. We drove around Beverly Hills, Hollywood Hills, and all the historical landmarks. We met with friends from Chicago, watched the Bears game, went to Venice Beach and ate great food. Ozzie's Uncle also lives in Laguna, so we met with him and took a boat out of Newport Beach. Then we drove to San Diego, went to the zoo, and met up with more friends. All in all, we had a great trip, and I think Nixon loves going on vacation! Not too shabby, if that will cure him from all of these hospital stays. We will just have to take monthly vacations!

November came and Nixon is able to spend his second birthday at home. Since we had that big bash in July for his transplant day, I decided to make it low key. We just have family over as our house isn't that big, but it is wonderful to be around loved ones in our own home celebrating such a special person. Nixon loved all of the attention. He had big smiles when we put his cake in front of him and sang. This is how I hope we celebrate every birthday. The day was just perfect.

The next few weeks, Nixon started having attacks/episodes about one to two times a day that were not seizures. He gets all jittery, almost as if he has flu chills and is sweaty and shaky. He had this back in September, which was the beginning and ultimately caused the really bad seizure that he had. The only medicine we can give him to stop them and calm him down is lorazepam. We give it to him right when we see it happen, so it doesn't get bad. One of the other Gaucher's moms reached out to me and actually asked me if Nixon had these described episodes. She told me that three other children with Gaucher's have the same episodes. Apparently, they are autonomic instability/storming episodes. She said that we should keep that under control because kids can get apneic which is when they stop breathing during their sleep. He is still having seizures when he falls asleep at night, but I have to say they are about 90% better than before and not as violent.

It took until December to play around with the medications before he was finally stabilized. On deck, in case we need it, we now have an oxygen tank, emergency medication for bad seizures, a suction machine, and ambu bags, which are self-inflating bags with a mask on it to administer CPR (so we don't have to use our mouths). We now feel more prepared and know what to do in case of an emergency. By mid-December, Nixon has eye surgery to correct his strabismus. It was an hour-long surgery. He had a few breathing problems, but was only in recovery for a couple of hours. As he opened his eyes, we noticed they were, in fact, straight! In addition to helping his vision, this corrective surgery will also help with any headaches he may have been having. I still can't believe that they cut my baby's eyeballs open. Thinking about it makes me queasy. But just like everything else, he came through it like a champ! Even though it has been quite a rough year for Nixon, he made it to his second birthday and ended the year on a high note. He is doing as well as he can be, and we are hoping that 2016 will be his year to thrive.

~

"What lies behind you and what lies in front of you, pales in comparison to what lies inside of you."

– Ralph Waldo Emerson

# Thirteen

THE BEGINNING OF 2016 was not what I expected. The more Ozzie and I think about it, we don't know if Nixon will end up being able to walk. We think he should be able to sit up on his own by now, if that were to ever happen. If he isn't able to sit up by now, it makes us wonder if his brain stem may have been affected by the disease. I still won't give up hope, as anything can happen. However, I am somewhat preparing myself for the possibility that he will never be able to walk. I keep forgetting that he missed a year of his life. During therapy exercises, I still work with him all the time and put him in his stander, but I just can't seem to get it right. I try so hard, and I feel like I'm not getting anywhere. I'm not a teacher, which is why I didn't become one, but I must teach him how to walk, talk, drink, sit, stand, and eat. His therapists only come for one hour a day. I feel like if he doesn't hit these milestones, then it's on me. I'm just exhausted. I'm trying to be a wife, a mother, a therapist (in all aspects), a housekeeper and a cook. I feel like I'm failing at everything. I'm usually able to try to find a solution to things, but I am at such a loss. I'm truly scared about what is going to happen. Sometimes, I think we are in over our heads. We were so passionate about saving his life, but we never thought about how we would be able to survive after the fact. I just cannot figure out a way on how we are going to be able to keep it all going.

We are scheduled to go back to Pennsylvania at the end of January. The more I think about things, the more I decide I must just take things one day at a time and try not to worry so much about the future. Otherwise, I will end up spending our good days getting stressed over something that we can't control. Something good has to come to us one of these days. It just has to.

The trip to Pennsylvania brought back so many emotions. It was such a life changing experience. Driving from the airport and walking into that hospital made me feel scared and sick, yet relieved and comforted all at the same time.

Our appointment with Dr. Escolar gave us time to hear her main concern about the seizures and the secretions (excess saliva) he has been having. She wants to adjust his medicine to see if that makes a difference; and then, we will just take things one step at a time. The therapist evaluation went well; they were very happy with his progress. He gained a lot development-wise, but it won't show in his charts because his development is slower than normal. He did lose a little bit in the fine motor skills category, but it could be because his eyes are still adjusting from surgery. His developmental stage is that of an 8-10-month-old. He is definitely maintaining the level he was at and even progressing in some areas; which is huge for a child with everything he endured in the last two years. Dr. Escolar said the next step is to promote his refluxes because it will tell us, eventually, if he will be able to walk. From a neurological standpoint, everything is stable.

Dr. Mark said his transplant numbers are awesome. His organs are as good as a normal human being. He is also still 100% donor! There is no trace of Gaucher's cells in his bone marrow, whatsoever. I asked him if we beat this thing. He said that we couldn't have done any better with his transplant, which made me cry. Now we just have to get these seizures and episodes under control. All in all, Nixon is doing amazing, and everyone thought he looked great and much healthier. Hooray for a successful trip to good ol' PA!

Over the next couple of months, Nixon's seizures started getting worse. They are so bad that we ended up in the hospital, and we were transferred to a children's hospital in downtown Chicago. This hospital is huge and beautiful, just like Pennsylvania. I have an eerie feeling inside of me that nothing about this situation is going to be good. My feelings have usually been right during this journey, so I have to prepare myself that we were going to be in for quite a ride. While in the pediatric unit, he seized so bad that they gave him twice his normal dose of medicine. It didn't even stop it. I decide I'm not leaving this hospital until I get answers and they fix him. I can't do this anymore. I'm so completely exhausted. I have slept six hours in three days and nothing we have tried is working. It takes all my energy to just keep him alive every day. Between the lack of sleep that he has endured and the seizures he has been having, I have no idea how or why he has the energy that he does. He still smiles all day long, grabs his balloons and shakes them in the air, and babbles away. Once again, he is flirting with all the nurses. I'm convinced that they transplanted him with vampire cord blood. He is not human.

The doctors order a spinal x-ray and a bone scan to see if the disease affected his spine and bones since the transplant. They said, if it is in fact the disease, then his brain could be so damaged that this could be the beginning of the end. Are you kidding me? He has come so far! I refuse to believe this, and it has to be something else. He has made so much progress and conquered so much that there is just no way.

We have learned that these storming episodes are brought on by discomfort so that is what we are trying to pinpoint. He did end up developing C-diff, which is a bacterial infection caused by antibiotics and causes severe abdominal cramping and pain. This could be what is causing everything. I'm actually banking on it. He was put on antibiotics a few weeks ago for possible pneumonia. They stopped the antibiotics, so we just have to wait and see.

My friend, Jamie and her husband, came to see us and stayed with Nixon for a couple of hours so Ozzie and I could get out. We went to a delicious chocolate store and had ice cream. Our next stop was a cheesecake restaurant where we grabbed a drink. It hit the spot, and I felt so refreshed. I started thinking more clearly and realized that there is just something that we are all missing; it's something so stupid that could be causing all of this; we just have to figure it out.

That night, I went down to the cafeteria to get something to drink. Before I left, the nurse was ready to deep suction him. I told her to do it with caution because sometimes he gets scared and clamps his mouth down. Both the nurse and Ozzie told me to take a break and get out of the room for a few minutes. He will be fine.

I made it down to the cafeteria when my phone rang. I saw it was Ozzie and my heart started pounding. He said, "Get up here right now." The elevator didn't move fast enough and I ran as fast as I could. When I turned the corner, I saw a crowd of people around our room and knew that it was a code blue. I made it to his room. Nixon is lifeless on the bed while the doctors and nurses are doing everything they can to get him to breathe. I asked Ozzie what happened, and it was exactly what I thought. He clamped down after being suctioned and just stopped breathing. They needed to get a breathing tube in him, but he started seizing. They had a very hard time opening his mouth. I became hysterical. I knew I shouldn't have left the room and at that second, I regretted leaving. My whole body started shaking uncontrollably, and I just curled into a ball on the floor. Ozzie called one of my friends who lived a few minutes from the hospital and asked her to get here as fast as she could because I was such a mess. He needed to be the strong one for Nixon and wanted someone to make sure that I was okay. I couldn't see what was going on. I just kept looking at Ozzie. He finally turned around and told me that they got the breathing tube in. They were taking him down to PICU, but I couldn't get myself to move. Ozzie went with Nixon and the medical team. I was just frozen on the ground. I couldn't believe that this happened again. My friend rushed into our room and just saw me on the floor with an empty room of just our belongings. I was hysterical. The look on her face……I knew exactly what she was thinking. I told her that he is alive, but they took him to the PICU. She ran over, hugged me, and started crying herself. Then she picked me up off the floor and started packing up our things.

When we arrived on the PICU floor, I walked into his room and saw him. He laid in his bed with the ventilator giving him his breaths. I immediately ran to the bathroom and threw up. The doctors told us that he is okay and he is stable. The plan is to keep him comfortable and get him strong enough so they can eventually try to extubate and get him breathing on his own. I couldn't help but think, how did I get here? How is this my life? How is it Nixon's? I have always been able to figure everything out, but I can't figure this out. This isn't fair.

I started looking back at some old pictures on my phone. In some, I have a huge smile on my face. I haven't smiled that big in forever. During those moments, my life was so good, and I had no idea what the future held. I'm lucky to have Nixon, and he is lucky to have me. I'm not sure what the reason is or why this happened but there has got to be a reason. Maybe I won't know for a long time, but some day, hopefully, there will be an answer to these questions.

A few hours pass and Nixon is already starting to fight. He opens his eyes a few times. It kills me to see him with that tube in his mouth. A bone scan and MRI are scheduled to hopefully get some answers about the storming episodes so we can get a plan to control them. The next few days are very critical. They need to figure out how to safely remove the ventilator, so he can breathe on his own without this happening again. He hasn't eaten because he can't have food right away after intubation, and he needs to have an empty stomach for tests. They put him on IV fluids. I'm concerned because these episodes take a lot of out of him, and he needs his strength. He is very strong and fighting very hard and wants to get through this.

The amount of time it takes for a baby to grow in a mommy's belly, is the same amount of time that I have spent breathing, eating, showering and sleeping in a children's hospital. And every day, there is no place else I would rather be than next to Nixon. Every morning, I wake up, and I fear that it is going to be the last day with my son. I try to make sure I look for my silver lining throughout the day. Four times a day, I hear that code blue alarm sound. I watch as the doctors and nurses scramble, and my heart falls into my stomach. I know the exact feeling that another mother is feeling at that moment. I don't wish that upon anyone. I don't have a great life. But I know that my life wouldn't be my life without Nixon. He has changed who I am and made me into a person who I never thought was ever inside of me. His smile is enough to make my day complete, and once I am able to see that, I can rest easy. I'm so happy that he is mine.

His tests came back normal. They couldn't find anything that could be concerning or causing any discomfort. Now, we are back to square one. The doctors felt that he was safe enough to take the tube out, so they extubated him. As soon as they pulled that tube out of his mouth he had a huge smile on his face! That's just what I needed to see. Not long after he was extubated, the episodes and seizures started again. I want them to start feeding him, so he can gain strength. They must wait for feeds for 24 hours after extubating. I started feeling very worried about how he would get through the episodes while being so weak. I wondered if these episodes happen because of the sedation medicine. Only time will tell as it starts to exit his system.

As the week went on, he wasn't sleeping much. His episodes continued. He still smiled from time to time, but the episodes were so frequent. I could tell how tired he was getting, and I didn't know how much longer he would be able to hang on. They started small feeds very slowly through his G-tube, but I knew it wasn't enough to give him the strength that he needed. Then one night, Ozzie and I passed out from exhaustion. One of the nurses we loved was working, so we felt it was a good night to try to get some rest. A few hours later, we woke up to the monitors going crazy. Both of us jumped out of bed. One of the doctors came in and asked, "What do you want to do?" since they haven't been able to figure out how to stop these episodes and currently don't have a plan. "What do I want to do!? I want you to save my child!" Lo and behold, they hook him back up to the ventilator. He has been through so much, and I was so torn up seeing him like this. But life has thrown so much at us. Despite how difficult things have been, we have survived. I have to trust that we can survive this.

The next day, Ozzie and I push the doctors to start feeding him. I told the doctors, if we want him off the ventilator again, he needs to get stronger to sustain these episodes. I knew deep inside that there was an answer for all of this; I just needed to figure it out. I needed time, but I was working against a ticking time bomb. The doctors were at a loss as at what to do and started telling us that his disease was getting the best of him. I immediately texted Dr. Escolar and updated her on what was going on. She texted back and said,

> "Do not get anxious; **let Nixon write his own story.** Many doctors don't know this disease, as it's so rare. I have not seen any sign of disease progression. It could just be a movement disorder like Parkinson's Disease. This could be his new norm, but it will take time to settle down. His body has been going through so much with two intubations. Movement disorders are hard to treat, but it doesn't mean that he is dying. He is a strong boy."

That night I struggled with whom I needed to believe. The doctors here were telling me it was disease progression, and we needed to start preparing ourselves. Dr. Escolar was saying the opposite. I sat on Nixon's bed and just begged for a sign to help get me through this. I focused my attention towards the TV and a baseball game was on. It was Chicago versus Pittsburgh. All of a sudden, the screen showed the entire beautiful city of Pittsburgh. That was my sign. I needed to listen to Dr. Escolar.

My second Mother's Day was upon me. This day is not about being a mom to a child. It's about that one thing that only women have inside of them, and it's indescribable. Somehow, and I don't know where we get it, but when it comes to being there for your kids, no matter the situation, there is something that God gave women. It's a strength to survive each day to take care of our kids and others, no matter if you have not slept or you, yourself feel sick. Today is very emotional for me. I don't know how things are going to pan out in the next days to come, but I'm just going moment by moment. Ozzie and I have only advocated for him, but Nixon has done all the hard work. He is the most amazing fighter that I have ever met and has strength like no other. He is a force to be reckoned with.

I was skeptical coming to this hospital because when Nixon was first diagnosed, we reached out to them. They weren't willing to help us because his disease was so rare and they felt it was untouchable. They said there was nothing that they could really do. However, when we were at our local hospital, they kept telling us to come here because they are the best. They can figure him out. Our insurance didn't want to send us here either, so we had to jump through hoops. On the ambulance ride here, I said to myself,

> "Maybe they will finally believe in him. Maybe they will see how strong he is, how well his transplant took and that he's worth fighting for. Maybe they will look past the whole 'Gaucher's Type 2 Stereotype' and look at the fact that he is engrafted, has been 100% donor since his very first chimerism test, and has not made a single Gaucher cell in almost two years."

Do I believe that this is a result of the disease? No doubt. We have always known that he would be affected from it. Last week, after they extubated him, Nixon was very weak and tired from not being fed for over a week. He was exhausted from having these movement episodes. I'm not sure why they are so skeptical about trying new things. I will not stop until I have exhausted every option I can find. He has not come this far for a movement disorder, muscle spasms, or seizures to take his life.

Ozzie and I thought long and hard. We decided that when they extubate him next time, if he has the same problem where the movements are not under control and they compromise his breathing, we will have him undergo a tracheostomy. This will create a surgical airway in the cervical trachea and means that instead of breathing through his nose and mouth, he will breathe through the trach in this throat. When he was diagnosed with Gaucher's Disease, we contacted every expert we could find. However, we have not spoken to any movement disorder specialists yet and we still want to try to pursue that.

We don't want him to suffer and have a bad quality of life. We want to make sure that we have all our options on the table before we make any rash decisions. We will read Nixon's signs, take one step at a time, and wait and see what he tells us.

I needed some normalcy from all of this, so I called in my troops. Two of my best friends came to the hospital that night. While we sat in Nixon's bathroom and chatted girl talk, they dyed my hair. This is what you resort to when you are living in a hospital.

After a few days pass, they gave Nixon some oxygen pressure support trials as they were preparing him to come off the ventilator. However, his x-ray didn't look that great and they wanted his lungs stronger before extubating. They didn't want to set him up for failure and wanted him at his prime. The doctors also decided that when they extubate him, they want ENT (ear, nose throat) doctors present so they can put a camera through his ventilator and see past his vocal cords. This way they can see how his airway reacts. As the camera is down there, they will remove the ventilator and slowly pull the camera out. If things go south and he has issues, they will be able to reintubate immediately. Ozzie and I feel better about this plan because they will get a better idea of what is going on with his airway, that is, if there is anything going on at all.

Thankfully, everything went smoothly and Nixon had a successful extubation. They put him on a CPAP machine to help open his lungs and make his breathing stronger. They have slowly been weaning his sedation medication and will continue to do so. He finally slept full nights and has been catching up on much needed sleep (2½ years' worth!). Nixon also slowly started getting feeds through his G-tube and they will gradually increase as he handles it. This little guy is the most amazing fighter and still has so much to prove!

Nixon finally reached a better place than he was a few weeks ago. Finally, I was able to hold him! It felt like the time when I held him for the very first time ever. It made me realize to never take holding him for granted. When your child is in pain, and you can't hold him, it is the absolute worst feeling you can ever feel.

We started talking with the doctors about moving Nixon from PICU to the regular floor. Huge step in the right direction! However, the night before the move, he started battling fevers, developed an upper respiratory infection, and his lung collapsed. I was so sure that we were closer to going home. Then his movements and seizure episodes started getting more frequent. I felt horrible for him because he was only having a few good moments throughout the day. I could no longer eat or sleep. Then, this really made me start thinking.

The doctors requested a care conference with Ozzie and me. This is a meeting where the doctors that have been caring for him share their thoughts with us, and we figure out a plan. As we walked down the hall to the care conference room, my heart wanted to jump out of my chest. I'm actually surprised I haven't had a heart attack yet. We are in unmarked territory with his disease, and I had no idea what they were about to say. As we sat around the table, they explained to us that they were at a loss. Nixon has gone through so much. Since he keeps going back and forth with his improvement they can't figure out how to make him stable and keep him stable. They were going to give him a week. If he doesn't show drastic improvement after a week then they wanted us to make some decisions. Ozzie and I agreed that we hate seeing him suffer. But I explained to the doctors that until I have exhausted every option that is out there, then I wasn't going to give up. I asked them about cannabis oil, which is a hemp oil that contains a significant level of cannabidiol, as well as essential vitamins, minerals, fatty acids, terpenes, flavonoids and other non-psychoactive cannabinoids. During my constant research, I read so many cases of how it helps so many children. They said it wasn't an option because it is so new and the clinical trials for it are currently ongoing. They were giving him a week, but they had no plan of how to help make him better, which made me angry. They weren't willing to try any new ideas. I know it has been really bad, but I can't even describe the amount of strength this child has inside of him. He has so much to prove in his life and has shown us that he is not finished with this life yet. I also know that I will know when it's time. I know that Nixon will show me, and he hasn't shown me yet.

The doctors continued to explain. If it came down to it, there are four options to let him go as peacefully as possible. I couldn't believe what I was hearing, and I couldn't believe they were having us make this decision. Ozzie and I both became numb and started crying. They asked if we wanted pictures taken at the time, if we wanted handprints and footprints, and who we wanted in the room when it happened. I felt empty. I wasn't thinking clearly, and I just couldn't even do this. Ozzie answered as best as he could because I could barely speak. I just wanted to get out of that room as fast as possible. When they brought us back to his room, Nixon was sleeping. I ran right to his bed, hugged and kissed him, and told him that he had to tell me if it was enough. I told him that I would do absolutely everything that I can possibly do for him, but he had to guide me through this. That I will never give up on him until he tells me that it is time.

Ozzie and I took a walk in the park across the street as we needed to talk things out and digest what had just happened. We sat in silence for a good ten minutes before either of us spoke. I told him that I'm not ready to give up yet and he agreed. We both decided that we didn't care what was said in that room. We were ready to move mountains for our child, and we had one week to do it.

We turned to the one thing that started us off on the journey at the very beginning. The internet. We found a reputable vendor and ordered cannabis oil, which was conveniently shipped to us. Every free hour, we researched as much as we could, so we could calculate the right dose to start. This wasn't a decision we made lightly, and we are not recommending it. In our situation, it was a matter of life or death; literally. And if we left it up to the doctors, we would be taking footprints and handprints in a week. We wanted to and had to give him every chance we could. No one was going to tell me what I can and can't do when it comes to my child. We had one week to pull out all the stops.

Cannabis (CBD) oil is an ingredient of marijuana, but not the illegal portion of the plant. CBD hemp oil is made from high-CBD, low THC hemp, unlike medical marijuana products, which are usually made from plants with high concentrations of psychoactive tetrahydrocannabinol (THC). Because hemp contains only trace amounts of THC, these hemp oil products are non-psychoactive.[1]

We started giving it to him when no one was in the room. This was our last Hail Mary pass. It had to work because if it didn't, then we would lose this war in seven days. A few days pass, and Nixon started to be more awake during the day. His fevers went away. As the doctors became more aggressive with his respiratory therapy, he went from high flow oxygen to regular oxygen. After one full week of giving him the CBD oil, Nixon was sitting up in a chair smiling. The doctors and nurses were shocked. Ozzie and I just shrugged our shoulders and said, "It's Nixon. He does what he wants to do."

After another week, they finally transferred us out of PICU onto a regular floor and prepared us for possibly going home. I was terrified to go home. I had no idea how I was going to do this by myself, but I knew that I had to. I couldn't just keep him in the hospital because I was scared. He came too far for that.

He needed to be home and be around everyone that loved him. He needed to start participating in life. We were given this life because we are strong enough to live it. I had to rip the band aid off and just do it. After 84 days in the hospital, they finally sent us home. I have to say that this hospital stay was worse than the seven months that we spent in good ol' PA.

[1]  Medical Marijuana, Inc. "What is CBD (cannabidiol) Hemp Oil?" http://www.medicalmarijuanainc.com/what-is-cbd-hemp-oil

~

"When you arise in the morning, think of what a precious privilege it is to be alive, to breathe, to think, to enjoy, to love."

– Marcus Aurelius

# Fourteen

**July, 2016**

NIXON IS AT HOME on continuous oxygen as well as a CPAP machine at night for apnea. He still has his movement episodes, but they are not as violent or life threatening as before. He did lose his ability to move his arms and legs from this last hospital stay. We believe it was because of the amount of sedation medication he was on, as well as, the fact he spent another 84 days in a hospital bed. Only time will tell whether he will regain it back with therapy. But his smile. His smile and laughs are everything. As long as he can engage and understand what life has to offer, that is all that matters! Since Nixon wasn't trapped in a hospital room anymore, we started living life. Friends came over for play dates. We went to the zoo. We took him for a haircut. He saw his first movie in a movie theatre about a fish that has memory loss. We went to a nearby racetrack to see the horses run. He did arts and crafts during therapy. We took walks to the park, and we went to a carnival. Since we missed all of spring and part of the summer, we started taking full advantage of the weather.

July 9th came. Nixon's 2nd re-birthday. Two years ago, on this day, Nixon was given a second chance at life. I will be forever grateful to his team of doctors and nurses in Pennsylvania. They gave us hope. Although we have had some major bumps in the road, without them, he would not be where he is today. This kid works so hard to do what comes naturally and easy for so many other kids. He finally started holding onto things again without help! He makes me so proud every single day. I was so happy to see him doing so well because it was time for the three-week follow up at the children's hospital in downtown Chicago. The team was so happy to see how well he was doing, and they told him to keep up the good work!

I literally have the most amazing kid. In September, he was supposed to have neurotoxin injections in his salivary glands to help with his secretions, but a few days before the surgery he told us that something wasn't right. He wasn't acting right, and it turns out that he had pneumonia. He ended up in a $CO_2$ coma. This causes elevated levels of carbon dioxide in his blood because he was not able to blow off enough of the $CO_2$ while breathing. Fortunately, we caught it before it became too dangerous.

While at our nearby hospital, Nixon was placed back on the ventilator, but it was a good thing because it helps bring his lungs back to where they need to be. Not long after, he was extubated. We hoped to have the neurotoxin injections done while we were in the hospital. That was until he bit his tongue so hard while he was having one of his episodes. It traumatized him enough into complete shock; he stopped breathing, and turned blue. Since the bleeding was so hard to control, the doctors were concerned that blood went into his lungs. He ended up getting reintubated. Luckily, the intubation was only a few days and he was extubated successfully. ENT was skeptical about doing the neurotoxin injections because he has been so fragile. We decided to postpone it, for now.

The child life program is amazing at this hospital. During a week of monitoring him, they brought a live fish tank to his room, and gave him a guitar. The doctors met with us to discuss the tracheostomy. He has been intubated so many times in the past few months they feel it will be a safer option for him. Ozzie and I always believed that if it came down to Nixon getting a trach, that we have failed him. He is the only child that we know with this disease that doesn't have a trach. We told them that we would consider it, but wanted to give him one more chance. Before this incident he was doing so great. I know he can get through this. He came this far and has more strength than a super hero.

Nixon's life is such a roller coaster ride. One minute he is doing great, and the next minute he has dipped towards danger. But he was given a chance at this life. He deserves the best chance that he can have, which is why we keep fighting. He keeps proving that he is going to fight as hard as he can to be here. My role in life is to be his designated hand holder, advocate and mom through this, and I wouldn't want to be anywhere else. I will try everything and do everything I can, so he can do as much as he can and be the best person that he can. So far, he has proven that he is beyond awesome.

At the beginning of October, we were released from the hospital. Settling in back home, our lives approached our new normal once again. We are now able to provide Nixon's respiratory treatments from home. A vibrating percussor is placed around Nixon's lungs twice a day to help keep them clear and strong. We deep suction him ourselves and give him the inhalers multiple times per day to keep his lungs open.

It took some time for Ozzie and me to get the hang of it. Soon it just blended in as a part of our normal routine. We want to keep our word to Nixon and do our best to avoid a tracheostomy. Ozzie was planning a fishing trip for the weekend, but the night before, Nixon just didn't seem right. He was doing great at first, and then around 11:00pm, I noticed his oxygen started dropping. I grabbed one of our home oxygen tanks and cranked it as high as it would go. I kept deep suctioning him, but nothing was coming out. We couldn't figure out why he wasn't keeping up his stats. We took him to the ER. Lo and behold, the chest X-ray showed his lung collapsed. I couldn't figure out why this kept happening. Why were his lungs so weak? They brought us to the PICU for the night and put him on high flow oxygen. The monitors indicated it was helping a lot. Maybe this was just a little bump in the road. I told the doctors that at home, we were doing everything we were told to do with his respiratory treatments. They explained that sometimes the lungs are just too weak and end up collapsing.

The next day he was much better. Ozzie went home to shower, and my friend came to the hospital for a visit. Nixon was napping peacefully on his belly as they wanted him off his lungs so that they could heal better. My friend and I were chatting until I noticed that Nixon started stirring a little. He opened his eyes very wide and smiled. I said, "Hi" and started rubbing his back. That was until I noticed he just didn't look right. I flipped him onto his back and realized he had stopped breathing. I grabbed the nurse. When she saw him, she said, "Hit the 'code blue' button on the wall." NOT. AGAIN!!!!! Immediately the alarms sounded, and everyone came rushing in. I just kept watching the monitors as his oxygen level plummeted from the 90's all the way down to 5. Then, for the first time ever, I saw his blood pressure and heart rate plummet. I became numb because at this point I thought I was really going to lose him. My friend grabbed onto me because I could barely stand since I was shaking so bad.

Luckily, Dr. Frank was in the hallway. He called Ozzie and spoke to him the whole way back to the hospital. All his stats rose to where they needed to be, but only for a minute until they started dropping again. The PICU fellow looked at me and told me that they were going to have to intubate him again. I told them to do whatever they had to do as we walked out in the hallway.

I was hysterical because it was that moment when I knew that Nixon was telling us that he needed a trach. What seemed like an eternity later, but was only 15 minutes, Ozzie came running down the hall. He looked right at me and said, "He needs a trach, doesn't he?" I just kept crying as he held me. Dr. Frank, whom at this point has become a part of our family, explained, "A trach will be a good thing. It doesn't have to be permanent. Nixon finally showed us that he needs it to help get him stronger." I felt so much comfort knowing that his pediatrician was there with us, and he felt that what we were going to do was the right thing.

Nixon settled comfortably with the ventilator. We quickly explained to the team of doctors that we decided we wanted to move forward with a tracheostomy. They were going to set it up for later that week. This disease is a roller coaster ride, but we will always continue to fight it. We feel this trach will help keep him much safer. Although we are deeply saddened that we will no longer hear his beautiful voice, it will protect his airway and hopefully give him a better quality of life. It doesn't have to be permanent. If I know Nixon like I do, he will get as strong as he can with his trach. Then, we can eventually have it removed, so one day he will be able to tell his own story. I cuddled up next to him on his bed and asked him to not be mad at us for making this decision for him.

The next day we wrote a social media post to share a status update with our family and friends about the trach. To my surprise, just about everyone that we knew changed their profiles to Nixon's picture in support of him this week. It opened my eyes so much. It showed me that life is not about stupid petty fights, money, politics, jobs, etc. It is about people. People who come together, who show support, who love each other no matter what. This situation shows that good in this life truly exists and supersedes anything negative. This child of ours is so unbelievably lucky. And he knows how lucky he is because he keeps fighting so damn hard, so that one day he can truly show the world his appreciation and what really matters.

On the morning of Nixon's trach surgery, I was a complete mess. When they took him out of his room, I just broke down, but I knew we made the right decision for him. His surgery lasted a few hours. When they brought him back to the room, I started bawling. It was nauseating seeing him with a trach in his neck and completely unconscious. They said he did well, and everything went as expected. When he woke up, he looked right at me and gave a little smirk. I told him that he would be able to breathe so much better now. The first night, he didn't sleep much, but his heart rate was much lower. I think it's because he could breathe better. It's definitely weird to think that he breathes through his neck now and not from his nose. He was still on pretty heavy pain meds, but I did get some smiles, which just melted my heart. I kissed his face just about a million times. I was finally able to get on the bed and snuggle with him, but I haven't been able to hold him yet. I miss holding him.

The trach will have to heal for about a week as everything in his throat must adjust and heal around it. They have it stitched in him. At the end of the week, they will take out the stitches and change out the trach. Back home, we will have to take it out once a week and clean it. This makes me want to vomit because there is a hole in his fricken neck. I have no idea how I'm going to do this. His ventilator settings will then have to be weaned to see if, in fact, he will need to be hooked up to a ventilator; and if so how long throughout the day. We also have to determine if he will need oxygen. We will start trach changes here at the hospital by ourselves, until we are comfortable. The next step is to coordinate schedules for home care nurses, once Nixon is at home. There will be more equipment. It's going to be overwhelming, and I'm scared, but there is no turning back now.

The next few days were rough as they had to take him off all his sedation drips and pain medicine. Hello, again, withdrawal. However, the bright side was the removal of the ventilator, and he no longer needed the CPAP. For two days and nights, he had to strictly be on a trach collar trial, which is just oxygen and a little bit of flow. He rocked it!

The next challenge was to get through his movement disorder episodes and his withdrawal that usually happens after he is on a ventilator. We worked with the home care team to exchange and add new equipment. We also scheduled the home nursing services. We hope to be in the hospital for another three weeks and be released November 7th, 2016, just past his 3rd birthday on November 1. The future was starting to look better. The best part was that finally, after almost three weeks, I was able to hold my baby again for the first time while he had his trach.

Once again, two steps forward, and five steps back. He spent the whole next week battling extremely high fevers. By high, I mean 106.7 plus instances where he stopped breathing. He caught a virus and infection, which is common when you spend so long in a hospital. They put a PICC line in for better IV access to administer medicine. The trach makes it easier to help him with his breathing. They also hooked him back up to the ventilator to give him more support. He opened his eyes for a brief second, and he even tried to talk over his trach. For the first time since his surgery, I heard his little voice. I was lucky enough that a few of my friends were visiting and my one girlfriend captured that moment. I'm so happy because it was a moment that I will never ever forget.

We made it to Halloween, and it was a week full of a lot of momentous events. I wasn't letting this stop him from celebrating, so I dressed my little man up as Mickey Mouse. My goodness was he adorable. Child life decorated his room, and the hospital put on a parade that walked by his room and everyone handed out treats. The next day was his 3$^{rd}$ birthday. Nixon was born at 12:45am on Nov. 1, 2013. I set my alarm for 12:40am, and the minute that it turned 12:45am, his eyes popped wide open. He looked at me and smirked. No WAY! He has taught me more in the three years that he has been on this earth, than I have learned in the 35 years that I have been on this earth. He has taught me to believe. He has taught me to hope. He has taught me that when you don't know what to believe in anymore, to look for signs and trust in them. We have been fighting this disease since the day he had been diagnosed. Dozens of doctors said he would not make it to his third birthday. Well, he did. We have fought and will continue to fight with every ounce of strength that we have.

The day after his birthday, the Chicago Cubs won the World Series. Although Ozzie is a huge White Sox fan, he let me put Nixon in a Cubs shirt and watch the game. Then, we came upon the crazy presidential election. Throughout my entire life, I have always worried about the future. One thing I have learned the past few years, which has kept me at peace, is to live for today and not worry about tomorrow. No one knows what is going to happen in the future. No one. You just have to believe, have hope, and have faith that one day all will be okay; until then, just live in the moment. And if today happens to be a hard day, and you get scared, don't run. You fight like hell to get through it, and just remember to keep loving.

We surpassed the date of discharge that they originally gave us. Nixon's episodes and fevers were not getting much better, and for a while we were at a loss. But then Ozzie and I started thinking clearly. We decided to go back to the basics from how we made it home this past summer. We spoke with the doctors, and we switched around some of his medicines and so far, it's been working! He started to become more awake and alert. He was sitting up in his high chair that we brought from home. We were even getting smiles. This has been the roughest year that we have had. This year, we have spent five months in a hospital. That is five months of sleeping in a chair, no home-cooked meals, living out of bags, and living in fear not knowing what the next minute is going to bring. We are coming up to Nixon's third Thanksgiving in a hospital. And as mad as I am that he hasn't experienced the tradition of being around a table with family, food and football, I'm still so extremely thankful. I'm thankful for the hospital staff that saved his life and makes him as comfortable as possible every day. I'm thankful that he is still with us. And most importantly, I'm thankful for the amazing support that we have received from family and friends through all of this. Sometimes, thank you doesn't even seem like enough. When life doesn't seem fair, I've learned to remember what is really important. And that is what I am truly thankful for this year.

Once December arrived, Nixon was getting better each day, and all our equipment was ready to go home with us. The nursing agency found one nurse for us. A couple of the nurses at the hospital said they would be our home nurses on their days off. We are extremely lucky. But Ozzie and I still had one unanswered question. It had been almost eight months since his last MRI. Since all these episodes were happening, we wanted to know what was going on with his brain. We begged the doctors for an MRI, since his last one was in April. It took some convincing, but they ordered it.

The MRI showed that he had cerebral atrophy, and his brain had shrunk drastically in the past eight months. This means that there is a loss of neurons and tissues in his brain similar to that of dementia. This explains why we have seen such regression in him this past year. We decide to take him home, so they discharged us before Christmas. We have no idea what is going to happen, but we know that taking him home will be the best option.

Before we arrive, our amazing friends transformed our house, so Nixon's room could be downstairs and we could take care of him on the first floor. We started Nixon with acupuncture and hippotherapy, which is when he rides on a horse once a week. We added hyperbaric oxygen therapy for 25 consecutive days where he sits in a chamber to receive high levels of oxygen greater than that of sea level atmospheric pressure. We even have a home exercise machine that mimics the movement of a horse, so he could have a form of hippotherapy daily. We are hoping these therapies are going to optimize him to the best of his abilities.

I reached out to a doctor in Japan who was doing a clinical trial for Gaucher's by using a cough tablet that is only available overseas. It helps carry the enzyme to the brain. Friends of ours who travel overseas get them for us. Nixon remains on cannabis and THC oil, which we obtain through his medical card that he is now prescribed. I have read many articles that it has benefits to help with any neurological progression. He is also on a cocktail mixture of vitamins that is known to help brain function.

After seven months of being home from the hospital, Nixon hasn't used the ventilator since January. He is completely off oxygen during the day. He is now off two of his Parkinson's medicines and is completely off his seizure medicine. We are doing something right because Nixon has been improving.

I will never regret putting Nixon through the stem cell transplant. After he received it, he no longer needed bi-weekly enzyme replacement therapy, it helped with his liver and spleen, and he made it past his third birthday. His brain was affected because Gaucher's Disease actually starts affecting these children in utero. Nixon didn't have his transplant until he was six-months-old, and the transplant doesn't even start taking affect until months after. Technically, he had over a year where the disease affected his brain. Nixon was born in November of 2013, and it wasn't until January 1st, 2014 that Gaucher's Disease was put on the newborn screening test in the state of Illinois. If we had known prior to his birth that he had this disease, and if I could do it all over again, then I would have chosen to transplant him right away.

My whole life, whenever something was broken, I would always say, "Well, fix it." I would always find a way, no matter what. I'm still that way. I'm still researching every single day, and I will always keep trying new things. I trust my heart and my gut more than anything in this world. My life motto is "Never, ever give up." I will always have hope because without hope you have nothing. And I will continue to keep the faith. Because of that, you never know when miracles will happen. I will treasure the small things, as they are the things that keep me going.

I have learned a lesson from this entire experience. Live your life. Don't worry about what could happen or what could kill you. Anything can happen to anyone for no apparent reason, whatsoever. And if an unfortunate circumstance happens, you find that inner strength and fight like hell.

The key to happiness is to let every situation be what it is, instead of what you think it should be. I never want to discredit any doctors, especially the ones that we spoke with, as they are only able to tell you what they know. But there is a reason why a parent is given such a thing as parental instinct. You need to follow that instinct, and always listen to what is in your heart. In the end, we live day by day. Sometimes hour by hour and sometimes minute by minute. We don't know what the future will hold, and that's okay. Sometimes it's better to not know because it makes you appreciate every day so much more. What it all comes down to is – you must make sure that you always fight for what you believe in. This little guy has proven to me that anything is possible, that life is worth fighting for, and most importantly, to never, ever give up.

~

"Every great dream begins with a dreamer. Always remember, you have within you the strength, the patience, and the passion to reach for the stars to change the world."

– Harriet Tubman

### Kristin Skenderi, Author

**Hearing a doctor say, "Your child is going to die,"** was the worst moment in Kristin Skenderi's life. Luckily, she is an eternal optimist and has never been one to take "no" for an answer.

"Every time a doctor tells me that my child is going to die, I reply, 'I hear what you are saying, but that is not going to happen. Until I have exhausted every single option in this world, I will not give in.' From that moment on, I keep it in the back of my mind. And every time I hear it, it just gives me the drive to fight harder."

Wife and Author, Kristin Skenderi, is also Champion Mom for son, 3-year-old, Nixon Skenderi. "Even when I was younger with anyone who was sad or sick, my response was, 'Okay, well, it happened; how do you fix it?' A lot of people get hung up on the 'why or how did this happen?' I say, 'who cares?' It happened. It doesn't matter, let's find a way to just fix it."

After growing up in Des Plaines, Illinois, Kristin graduated from Illinois State University driven to achieve great success in sales. She worked very hard at it and excelled amongst her colleagues. Her high school classmate, Ozzie Skenderi, graduated from Western Illinois, and the two married in 2012. Soon after, in 2013, Nixon was born, and Kristin planned to and wanted to return to work.

"When he was diagnosed, and I realized our lives were changing, my constant need to be busy, to work, to have job security, money and everything else went out the window. My sole focus was about him. I was and still am determined to do anything I can possibly do to save Nixon's life."

To find the 'right solutions,' Kristin asks questions and takes copious notes. "I think we live in a world today that gives us so many options. We just have to keep looking. I always argue my way until I feel that I have found the right solutions."

"When the doctor is talking to us and giving us all types of information, we are not really 'listening' to what he/she is saying. I use my notes later when I have time to read and digest the notes, research more and assess the following:

- Here's what they are saying.
- Here's what they are saying can be done.
- I think outside the box and ask, 'Is there another way? If we all worked together, maybe there is a better solution.'
- Then I ask, 'Am I well-informed; what is my instinct telling me; and does this 'feel' like the right approach?'"

There has never been a time when Kristin and Ozzie have felt they were going to throw in the towel and give up. They always wondered about how or if they would know. A good friend whose son had the same diagnosis shared, "You will just know. I can't even describe it to you. Nixon will tell you. He will tell you, 'It's time. I'm done.' And you will know."

"Every time we try something new or we are going through a process, I look at Nixon's face, his eyes, his demeanor. For the more difficult decisions, I say, 'You have to guide me through this.' Never once has he told me to stop. His strength and will to live drives me every day. He is the strongest person I have ever known."

~

**Now that you have read the book, keep updated with Nixon's journey!**

**Facebook –** Search Nixon's Fight #NixonStrong
https://www.facebook.com/Nixons-Fight-Holding-Hope-in-our-Hands-474937502650185/